# How to Manifest Money Effortlessly

## Techniques to be More Prosperous

# How to Manifest Money Effortlessly

## Techniques to be More Prosperous

Dr. Bruno Cignacco PhD

BOOKS

Winchester, UK
Washington, USA

First published by O-Books, 2013
O-Books is an imprint of John Hunt Publishing Ltd., Laurel House, Station Approach,
Alresford, Hants, SO24 9JH, UK
office1@jhpbooks.net
www.johnhuntpublishing.com

For distributor details and how to order please visit the 'Ordering' section on our website.



ISBN: 978 1 78279 082 2



A CIP catalogue record for this book is available from the British Library.

Design: Stuart Davies

Printed and bound by CPI Group (UK) Ltd, Croydon, CR0 4YY

# CONTENTS

*Riches are of the mind. Let us suppose for a moment that a physician's diploma was stolen together with his office equipment. I am sure you would agree that his wealth was in his mind. He could still carry on, diagnose disease, prescribe, operate, and lecture... Only his symbols were stolen; he could always get additional supplies. His riches were in his mental capacity, knowledge to help to others, and his ability to contribute to humanity in general.*

*Joseph Murphy*

# The Author

Dr. Bruno Roque Cignacco (PhD) studied Metaphysics for more than 15 Years. He wrote a business book "Fundamentals of International Marketing. SMES" 2010 (Atlantic Publishers) also published in Spanish and Portuguese. He also published a novel called "El niño errante (The Wandering Child)" (2010), Bergerac Ediciones.

The author is also a University Professor both at undergraduate and postgraduate level in business subjects in the UK and an international speaker and advisor on International Business topics. His e-mail is bcignacco@yahoo.com

# Acknowledgements

This book is dedicated to the memory of my Mother who was the person who first introduced me to the metaphysical principles which have deeply influenced this book.

I am also deeply grateful to:

- Fayola Saunders, a very sweet and special person in my life who showed great enthusiasm in reviewing the manuscript

- My Father, my Sister, my Niece and my Godson.

- My Uncle Hugo Francesconi, for his continuous support and faith in me.

- My Friends.

- My Clients.

- The people working for John Hunt Publishing for their significant support during the publishing process.

# Purpose of this Book

*Like water money is a carrier. It can carry blessed energy, possibility or intention, or it can carry control, domination and guilt.*
*Lynne Twist*

Money affects every aspect of your life, you cannot deny this. Throughout history we can see that money has been the main factor underneath many negative events such as war, slavery, exploitation, environmental pollution, unemployment and human traffic, among others. But, at the same time, money has also propelled positive events such as the discovery of new drugs, technological advancements, charity activities, and the development of new infrastructure, among others.

So you can see that, from a practical perspective, money is only a means to an end. Like a tool, it does not have intrinsic value in itself. The value that we assign to money depends on its specific use. The value we attach to money is intimately related to its varying meanings.

You are always dealing with money, in some cases in an ineffective way. Sometimes prosperity seems to be the privilege of only a chosen few. Throughout this book you will see that this is not true. Everybody is capable of being prosperous. But if you want to be affluent, you have to use the right tools.

This book will provide you with useful guidance to attract money in an effortless manner. This is not the traditional knowledge that you read in economic or investment bibliography, although that can be useful too. This text is more focused on non-traditional techniques to generate abundance in your life.

This text boils down the most relevant metaphysical principles related to the creation of wealth. The correct application of these rules will benefit you financially. These inexorable principles, which were exposed by the enlightened over centuries, will improve your life as a whole. These changeless laws will also enhance your mental flexibility and discernment about money.

As you go through this text you will progressively get familiar with the process of generating prosperity. Each of the topics explained in this book will be accompanied by very simple exercises to attract money ceaselessly. These universal techniques now can be at your fingertips at any moment and on any occasion. When you apply these instruments, you are dealing with eternal immutable silent forces, which are more powerful than you can ever imagine.

All strategies detailed in this text will also expand your belief system. As a consequence, you will feel more capable in creating miraculous circumstances regarding money issues. You will soon find out that, with the right application of the knowledge enclosed in this book, all your monetary needs will be met with no struggle. You will be amazed by the way your financial problems are solved spontaneously and gracefully. However, always be aware that this will not be a miracle. Your prosperity will be the natural outcome of tapping into the universal forces, which are always fair and effective. Rest assured that these acorns of wisdom will greatly help you achieve financial prosperity.

# Section 1

## General Aspects of Money and its Manifestation

*Money is a current, a carrier, a conduit for our intentions. Money carries the imprimatur of our soul.*
*Lynne Twist*

This section sets out wrong assumptions about money and positive connotations about it. This section also explains the Law of Attraction. It also highlights the main requirements to attract more abundance.

# Chapter 1

## 1. Wrong assumptions about money

*Nothing can happen to use unless it happens through us. That which we refuse to accept, to us, cannot be, and that which to us is, cannot help becoming a reality in our minds.*
*Ernest Holmes*

*Scarcity is a lie. Independent of any actual amount of resources, it is an unexamined and false system of assumptions, opinions, and beliefs from which we view the world as a place where we are in constant danger of having our needs unmet.*
*Lynne Twist*

### General aspects

You probably realise there are a lot of false assumptions, albeit very well accepted, about money. Those money "principles" are generally rife in our society. Most of these assumptions are well known by all people.

It's very likely that you have heard these remarks from parents, friends, media, institutions, and so on. These are generally presented as truisms. However believing in these assumptions only pushes you away from prosperity. You have to understand that these premises are completely detrimental; they prevent you from attracting more affluence in your life. Some of the false assumptions about money are:

- Money is the root of all evil
- It takes time to make money
- It takes a lot of effort to make money
- To earn more money I have to work more
- It's not polite to talk about money
- There is no virtue in having money

- You need money to make money
- People with abundant money are unhappy
- Save money for the rainy day
- There is not enough money
- Time is money
- People with money have specific skills
- You were not born to have money
- If I have more money I will have an easier life
- Money can't get you happiness or health
- There's a limit to the money you can earn
- Money is hard to get
- You have the money you deserve
- Money is king
- People with money are immoral
- The one who has more money wins
- People with money are stressed
- It's difficult to manage a lot of money
- Money is dirty
- People with money are different
- Money makes the world go around
- Money corrupts people
- If I have more money I will be ripped by taxes
- If I have lots of money, I may lose it
- I cannot be spiritual with a lot of money
- How can I have more money when others have very little?
- If I have more money people will resent me or hate me
- I haven't had too much money in the past so I cannot change
- You cannot fulfil your mission with plenteous money
- If I earn a lot of money, people will only be interested in my money
- You cannot have more money in the current economic situation
- If I get a lot of money I will dismiss other areas of my life
- It's not good to have more money than your progenitors

- People with a lot of money are superficial, egotistical and vain

It's very likely that you, like most of the people, accept those commonplaces without challenging them. Many people believe in those ideas because other people do. According to Cialdini certain tenets are ingrained in our society because of a principle of social proof, which states "*we determine what is correct by finding out what other people think that is correct*"

All these assumptions, albeit trite, might be deeply rooted in your subconscious mind. Over this book you will discover that none of these statements are true. On the contrary, all these ideas are absolutely fallacious.

You should review each of these statements critically. Try to discover why they are not "absolute truths". It is important to realise that all these premises about money are primarily based on trepidation, doubt and fear. All those sayings are stated from a perspective of scarcity thinking or *poverty mindset* that most people have.

If you analyse those ideas thoroughly you will see that those sayings are just justifications preventing you from having more money. These negative statements only create immense resistance to attract prosperity. It's about time you cleansed your belief warehouse from those detrimental ideas. By dispelling them, or at least questioning them discerningly, you will find the path to a more prosperous life.

## Exercise

Remele suggests a very interesting exercise in order to counteract those unproductive statements. In each statement, you have to replace the word "money" by a term with less intense connotations such as "shovels". For example the sentence "Money corrupts people" should be replaced by "Shovels corrupt people".

Repeat the exercise with each of the previous sentences. The objective of this exercise is to empty these statements from their erroneous meaning.

## 2. Positive connotations about money

*It's a currency or creative flow of divine activity.*
*Eric Buttenworth*

### 2.1. General aspects

There are many meanings attached to money. You can find below some useful connotations about money. Be aware that most people will tend to offer resistance to these positive connotations for different reasons: attachment to negative assumptions about money, scepticism, fear of change, undeservedness, wariness, among others.

- Money is a symbol
- Money is malleable energy
- Money is a signal of your growth
- Money is the reward to your added value
- Money is the Universe's unlimited provision
- Money is abundant matter
- Money is a result of your thoughts
- Money is effortless manifestation
- Money is a symbol of prosperity
- Money is a consequence of your intention
- Money is freedom and independence
- Money is living spiritual substance
- Money is an extension of who you are
- Money is love manifestation
- Money is omnipresent
- Money is a reflection of your inner state
- Money is a medium of exchange

- Money is a circulating commodity
- Money is an emotional issue
- Money is a tool for your goals
- Money is a friend
- Money is pure joy and fun
- Money is a multiplier of resources
- Money is almighty will
- Money is the pathway to deeper experiences
- Money is your power within
- Money is limitless
- Money is a means not a destination
- Money is my servant not the owner
- Money is an enabling resource
- Money it a test for your attitude
- Money is a sign of your confidence
- Money is something to be enjoyed
- Money is a wonderful idea
- Money is an act of faith
- Money is a facilitator for your inspired actions
- Money is the lively river of life
- Money is the value of goods or services
- Money is an amicable partner
- Money is all good

## 2.2. Exercise

Ask yourself the following questions. Write down the answers and read them critically.

How do each of these positive meanings resonate in your mind?

Are those connotations challenging your longstanding beliefs? If so, explain how. If not, explain why not.

What are the benefits of incorporating these affirmative meanings to your current belief system?

# Chapter 2

# Requirements to Attract Prosperity

*There are certain laws that govern the acquisition of riches, once these laws are mastered and applied, riches follow with mathematical certainty.*
*Robert Russell*

## 1. The Law of Attraction

### 1.1. Your thoughts are almighty

*Your outer world of form and experience is a reflection of your inner world of thoughts and feelings.*
*John Randolph Price*

*The **Law*** **of Attraction** states that you attract everything you desire, either good or bad. This law always applies. At all times you manifest what you wish, either negative or positive. From this perspective, you are the only cause of everything that occurs in your life. For this reason, you have to be very careful with the thoughts that you have in your mind.

Although you may not have realised, you are continually creating with your thoughts. For this reason you should be responsible with your thinking. All your current circumstances, relationships, money and other belongings, health conditions and work activities are just the results of your thoughts. There isn't anything that exists in your life that is incongruent to your thoughts. To put it simply, everything that is around you, all things you own or get in contact with are drawn to you because of your thinking. Sometimes you attract things deliberately and others unwittingly. Nevertheless your external situation is always a literal reflection of your internal state.

You habitually use your mind to attract both beneficial things and detrimental ones. You will argue, of course, that you want only to attract positive things, not detrimental ones. For example, you will say that you want to attract more money. You surely have many reasons to be prosperous such as working less, devoting your time to your favourite activities, travelling all over the world or helping other people or buying more clothes, houses or cars, among others. You probably ask yourself: *"How can I be asking for negative economic circumstances in my life?"*

It's important to highlight that each time you complain or moan about you financial conditions, or say "no" to it, you unwittingly attract the same negative circumstances (that you want to get rid of) to your life. From the metaphysical perspective you cannot push things away only attract them. For this reason it's necessary to focus on only positive things. For example, you should be focused on being more prosperous, not less poor. You should also appreciate what you have in your life, which most of the time you may take for granted, and be grateful about it. If you focus on the good things that you have in your life you will undoubtedly attract more abundance in your life.

Some sages use a very interesting metaphor to explain your unlimited mental power. You can manifest what you want in your life in the same way as if you were selecting a dish at a restaurant. In this case, you look at the menu, you look at the courses of your preference and you order it. That's it, you don't need anything else. In the same way, this is applicable to your mental capability. You should focus your attention on things you desire, you energise those images with positive emotions and the universal forces will certainly bring them to you.

Many people tend to act on the external negative conditions, trying to change them, in some cases, forcefully. From the metaphysical perspective, change is an inside-out process, you modify your thoughts and as a natural result, your conditions will change.

## 1.2. Everything vibrates

*Take control of your thoughts and feelings, they are the blueprint of your life.*
*Herbert Harris*

There is another important point to pinpoint. Everything you see in this world is made up of energy, which is vibrating at different levels. Even the things that look still are vibrating on a molecular level. Your thoughts and emotions are energy too, with a specific vibration. You must realise that you are naturally a vibrational being.

The vibrations of thoughts always attract things of equivalent or corresponding vibrations, such as specific people, things, events, etc. Your thoughts are extremely powerful because they manifest what you think about intently and consistently. You can create anything by design. Your power is, in fact, limitless.

This is not only a metaphysical assertion; Quantum Physics has discovered this too. The universe is an unlimited malleable field of energy. Our thoughts and feelings are energy too affecting the universal field to bring forth things into manifestation.

Scientifically speaking, quantum physicists say that the act of observing things is actually what prompts them to be. From a quantum perspective, everything in the universe is made of waves of energy. It is your observation that converts them into specific particles with a given location and time. However if you don't focus your attention, they become waves again. This means that all definite things only exist because of your observation, they cannot exist by themselves.

The Law of Attraction works perfectly when you follow a specific set of requirements. When you want to attract money, your attitude is very important. We will analyse the attributes of a prosperous mindset. With this mindset it will be easier for you to manifest more money flowing into your life. Find below the principles to apply the Law correctly.

## 2. Requirements to apply the Law of Attraction
### 2.1. Self-confidence and patience

> *The fastest way to be confident? Act as if you were confident. The mind cannot tell the difference between something that happens in reality and something it imagines with emotional intensity.*
> *David Taylor*

In order to manifest your desires, you must believe in your uncharted resources. You should have the innocent and naive confidence of a child. You are a spiritual being with immense power. You have the same essential characteristics of the Universe itself.

You are unbounded and almighty, regardless of your past negative conditioning. Everything you truly desire is possible; all your dreams will manifest if you believe in your own power. You are a God-like being with infinite endowments. However most of these resources are usually under-utilised or unknown.

You are the manager of universal boundless forces. You are a powerful conduit channelling energy to manifest any form possible. You must know the invisible universal power that brings all things into manifestation goes through you.

You must rely on your own limitlessness, be confident that you will succeed in any endeavour you take. However it is very important not to confuse confidence with arrogance. Confidence is trusting in something or somebody unreservedly. On the contrary, arrogance is showing an overrated self-worth and generally despising others. Confidence is always uniting, but arrogance is divisive.

You must be confident that your dreams will materialise. However your desires cannot be manifested easily when you feel anxious. Any state of eagerness or tension must be left aside for things to turn up. For this reason, you should relax physically, emotionally, and mentally. A state of relaxation will help you turn your desires into material things. Stressing situations or circumstances should be faced calmly or avoided if that is possible. Even the most problematic events in your life should be approached in a serene manner.

The states of tension, angst and anxiety are detrimental to attracting prosperity. When you are uptight, fretful or distressed you are pushing affluence away. You are generating negative vibrations that are incongruent with the manifestation of your dreams.

For this reason, it is advisable for you to relax on a frequent basis. In this book you will find some meditation techniques that can be useful for that. The more calm and patient you are, the quicker your desires will manifest. Wolhorn wisely states that *"tension and hurry delays the demonstration"* of your desires and *"in quietness and confidence shall be your strength"*.

In relation to the above mentioned, it is important to know that the manifestation of our desires is very unlikely to be immediate. Any delay regarding your objects of desire does not mean that they will not materialise at all. You have to understand that the Universe always has the perfect timing to bring about the desired things into your life.

There is another reason why anxiousness is detrimental for the manifestation of your dreams. The manifesting process falters in the presence of neediness, nervousness or hastiness because you are disconnected from the universal flow. When you are anxious you can't access the universal provision, which naturally cares for all your desires.

For this reason you should perform activities that put you in a calming state. In this way, some activities such as listening to soothing music, sessions of massage, acupuncture, yoga or meditation are very good. When you are relaxed you generate high vibrations that contribute to the materialisation of your desires.

Lastly you don't need to make the achievement of your goals into an effort. You must realise that "effort" represents strain and resistance and generates negative vibrations. From the metaphysical perspective, trying hard is not the best way to achieve your objectives. You should never become worn out, either mentally or in your actions. This does not mean that you never have to take actions. You can act, but only in an inspired and effortless way, when it is necessary.

Any effort made pushes any potential manifestation astray. Instead, effortlessness is totally compatible with the materialisation of your dreams. In conclusion the most important factors for the materialisation of your desires are: relaxation, composure and reliance on the almighty provision of the Universe.

## 2.2. Faith

*If you fix upon consciousness the fact that the desire you feel for the possession of riches is one with the desire of the Omnipotence for more complete expression, your faith becomes invincible.*
*Wallace Wattles*

You can only experience affluence when you rid yourself of any doubt. Trepidation and lack of faith are totally incompatible to the manifestation of abundance in any aspect of life, even money and material things.

All things are manifested when you steadfastly believe in the unseen. You should be confident in the manifestation of your desires before this happens. It's important to leave your incredulity and scepticism aside. The manifestation of the desired things is based on unfaltering faith. According to Copeland *"faith is a spiritual force, a spiritual energy, a spiritual power"*.

In order to materialise your desires you should "believe to see". In this way you are confident despite not having any concrete evidence of the materialisation of your dreams. You should never act the other way around, "see is to believe", that is a situation in which you believe once your desires have manifested.

Every time you use the visualisation techniques, which will be explained later in this book, you focus on things which are not still there. When you visualise you are envisioning the objects of your desire, but they have not materialised yet. Visualising is considered to be one of the most powerful ways to attract the things you want.

If you want to attract prosperity, you should have unwavering confidence in the almighty provision of the Universe. You must realise that the Universe is abundant by nature and can provide you with whatever you desire. This is the same omnipotent force that forms the tides of the seas, brings trillions of beings to life and makes our planet turn.

In order to receive from the universal supply you should have an open attitude. It's important to be willing to receive its gifts. Your faith in the universal forces must be unshakable.

Be aware the Universe will always take the path of efficiency to meet your expectation. The universal forces act with no resistance to fulfil your most cherished desires. Your dreams will be materialised in the best way, in the ideal time.

It's important to realise that fear is also faith, but applied in a negative way. When you are fearful, you focus on unwanted things and you believe that they will happen. Fear not only creates resistance against the materialisation of your desires, but at the same time attracts the very thing you fear.

There is another important point to highlight. In order to attract what you want, you should always have an attitude of detachment from the result. Attachment is a synonym of fear, anxiety, forcefulness and doubt. Each time you show desperation or extreme eagerness regarding the things to be manifested, you push the desired object away. You are generating negative vibrations that are inconsistent with the materialisation of your desires.

For this reason, the most appropriate state for manifestation is detachment. This means that you want things to be manifested, but you are not overly eager or worried about them. When you have a detached attitude you can live without the objects of your desire in the case that they did not show up. This appears to be counterintuitive but when you have an unworried attitude regarding your dreams, they materialise even faster.

Attachment obstructs the manifestation of your desire because an overly intense desire is generally related to lack. When you experience a state of scarcity, you are radiating negative vibrations that bring about more lack in your life. In order to be detached you have to be sure that all your desires will be fulfilled in the best fashion, at the right time and with the ideal resources.

When you have sterling faith, your unlimited mind power converts your abstract thoughts into definite objects. But also when you have faith you surrender to the almighty forces of the Universe, you become more receptive to the gifts to be provided by the universal flow.

When you have faith you don't have to understand how the Universe will manifest your desires; the universal forces have their own ways. The limitless provision of the Universe will organise means and time for your desired objects to come into manifestation. You do not have to think about how the desired things will come to you. How things will manifest is the Universe's domain.

Rest assured that universal forces will orchestrate the manifestation in the best way possible. For this reason, you should always focus on the end results not on the means. For example, if you visualise having £1,000,000 in your bank account, don't try to figure out how this will happen. Trust the universal forces, they will find the best means for this money to materialise. The universal supply is unlimited by nature and uses means that you cannot even imagine. The omnipotent Universe will choose the best means, the most appropriate resources and the most adequate people and ideal timing to fulfil your objective. For this reason, you should focus on the final product, not on the process of its development (or means).

It's important that you don't have any hesitation regarding the things that you desire. You must know that doubts are the main blockages in the process of manifesting your dreams. In fact, doubts always create intense resistance to the materialisation of your desires.

When you doubt the universal supply, you are conveying a confusing message. With your hesitative attitude you are implicitly telling the Universe you are not completely sure about your desires, because you have doubt about their materialisation. So the Universe will act on that, not providing those things you fervently desire. Each time you hesitate, you are shooting at your feet, because you push the things you desire far away.

For this reason, you must always have positive expectations about the upcoming things. These expectations are different from obsessive thoughts; the former are correct, the latter are totally counterproductive. It was explained before that restless rumination about your desired things creates discomfort and resistance, which pushes those very things away. Moreover a state of obsession or preoccupation about your dreams never puts you in alignment with the Universe, which makes it impossible to receive those desired things.

You must always believe that the frictionless, effortless and unfaltering means of the Universe will meet your expectations, even your wildest dreams. Don't settle for anything less than your innermost desires; always believe that they will be fulfilled. However be aware that you will find that some people will not agree with your new attitude. Don't pay attention to them, and rest assured that your dreams will come true.

So take your mind off anything or anybody that can quench your faith. Don't pay attention to people questioning your desires. Be serene and with positive expectations. Your unwavering expectancy will hasten the manifestation process.

Lastly don't give up if your desires have not been manifested yet. The universe has its own ideal time for the desired things to show up. Your faith places you in the same wavelength as the universal unbounded supply. As a consequence your desires will be materialised accordingly. Imagine faith as the consent you give to the Universe about the things you believe you deserve.

## 2.3. Positive emotions

*When our thinking and feeling are wrong – then we make it... impossible for 'things' to work correctly on 'the outside.*
*Charles M. Simmons*

In order to manifest more abundance in your life, you should always dwell on positive feelings. It's important to avoid, whenever possible, any negative emotion. You have to understand that your negative feelings only create resistance to the manifestation of your desires.

Sadness, confusion, envy, hatred, disappointment, harsh criticism, guilt and resentment are blatant examples of emotional states extremely incompatible with the manifestation of more prosperity. All these states offer intense resistance to the materialisation of your desires. All these emotions have a very low vibration, which will hinder your progress. These states, instead, draw to you detrimental things (for example, scarcity or lack), which have a like vibration.

On the contrary, joy, peace, enthusiasm, deservedness, happiness, playfulness and plenitude are examples of emotional states that accelerate the manifestation of your wishes. When you experience these emotional states you are aligned with manifestation of more affluence in your life.

When you visualise the objects of your desires, it is important to experience good emotions. When you use visualisation you should feel as if you were in possession of the desired things, although they have not manifested yet. For example, if you want to have £1,000,000 in your bank account you can imagine touching and reading the bank statement with that balance. You can also imagine buying things, such as a house or car, with that money. You can also experience in advance the feelings of joy and happiness of having that money in your account. You should imagine things as if your desires have been fulfilled.

It was explained that you always watch your thoughts, to hold only positive ones. However sometimes it is very difficult to examine all your thoughts, you have thousands of them a day. For this reason, many masters suggest that, instead, you should have a look at your emotions.

From this perspective your feelings are very precise predictors of what is on the way to manifesting in your life. Your feelings radiate vibrations, either high or low, which will attract like things and situations. If your emotions are positive (enthusiasm, joy, etc.) you are on the way to materialise good things. However if your feelings are negative (sadness, anger, etc.) you will not only resist the manifestation of positive things, but also attract counterproductive ones.

For this reason, it's important that you should engage in activities that prompt you to feel positive emotions. Some activities that can uplift your feelings are: going on holiday, watching comedies, reading self help books, listening to pleasant music, dancing and practicing sports, among others.

A second important factor to take in to account is forgiveness. You must always forgive yourself and other people, especially in relation to situations in which you experienced scarcity. In the past you might have gone through financial blunders, loss of money or plain scarcity. People that cheated on you regarding money might have been employers, employees, clients, suppliers, partners, creditors, debtors, friends, beaus, relatives or acquaintances. You may include in that list any organisation you were in contact with or the government. These people might have taken advantage of you, causing you to lose money, not to earn enough or to manage it improperly.

It does not matter if these people are still alive, if you are in contact with them or not. In any case, you should forgive them from the depth of your heart. Heartfelt forgiveness always unblocks your path to prosperity. When you harbour grudges against people that stole, exploited or deceived you regarding money, you are hindering the way to manifestation of your desires. Once you forgive these people, you should send them love and let all those memories go away. This will drastically change your vibration from a negative one (non-forgiveness, hatred, etc.) to a positive one (love, forgiveness).

This important technique helps you detangle some of the unsolved issues related to money. This tool also provides you with much more energy to manifest your wishes. With the application of this technique you cleanse your energy system from residual negative emotions. That makes you more open to receive the object you desire.

Besides, you should also forgive yourself. You should be compassionate about any wrongs you have done in relation to money. Always forgive the mistakes you made and the opportunity you lost concerning money. You should never punish yourself for your mistakes. In the past you have done the best possible with the resources available at that moment. Now you are a different person, with a much more evolved mindset, more conscious of your limitlessness.

By having a compassionate and non-judgmental attitude you clear out negative emotions that block the way to prosperity. You have to understand that rancour and resentment to yourself or others is a defensive measure, albeit a harmful one, you adopt, like most people. However those negative emotional states are not beneficial for your serenity of mind. Neither are they for the manifestation of your desires. So forgiveness is the most effective manner to clear them out.

## 2.4. Other factors

*How you think about money determines exactly what your financial reality is.*
*Dr Stuart Grayson*

Other factors that favour the manifestation of your desires are the abundance mindset, the stability of focus and secretiveness.

It's important to have a mentality of abundance. This perspective implies being aware that prosperity is present everywhere; you can always be prosperous. However economic news and the media in general tend to promote the opposite; they support the idea that you live in a world of poverty, unemployment and insecurity. Believing in their scarcity message is totally counterproductive. Their ideas are detrimental to attract abundance; you will not be able to manifest prosperity if you believe in lack.

There is another important point to highlight. According to abundance perspective for your dreams to manifest, you don't need to take any resources from anybody else. When you become rich other people will not necessarily become poorer because universal resources are limitless. There are enough resources to materialise everyone's desires.

From an abundance perspective, world resources will never become exhausted, even when all people attain their own objectives. That means scarcity does not exist. Lack is a human collective fabrication, a fear-based invention. Everyone is able and deserves to obtain everything they desire.

A second point to analyse is stability of focus. Whenever possible, hold a vivid image in your mind of the objects or situations you want to manifest in your life. You must be very concentrated on the object of your desire, as if you lost track of yourself in the process. If your desire is having more money, see in your mind's eye the notes, bank statements and cheques with big amounts. This technique is called visualisation and it will be explained in detail later in this book.

When you visualise your desires you should be consistent. Once the images of the desired things are formed in your mind, you should be totally congruent with them. You should not be focusing on the existent conditions, that is to say things you lack at the present moment. For example if you want to have £1,000,000 in your bank account, you should not be paying attention to your current bank statement balance of £5,000. On the contrary, try to imagine that your bank statement actually has £1,000,000. When you hold this image frequently and congruently it will tend to manifest in reality.

To put this simply, the primary focus of your thoughts should always be the things about to come. You should visualise them, as if they were here at present, using lifelike imagery and positive emotions. As a priority, your focus must be on what is on the way to manifest. So do not concentrate on the undesired current situation.

When you complain or moan about your problematic situation (for example, your current lack of money) you are not focusing on the desired things (for example, having more money). So if you focus on lack, you will manifest more lack. You cannot manifest prosperity when you focus on scarcity.

When you apply the Law of Attraction the negative sentences (for example, in statements like "I don't want to be poor" or "I don't want more debts") are interpreted as positive ones by the universe ("I want to be poor", "I want more debts"). So always focus on what you want, and not on what you don't desire in your life. Beware that, according to the Law of Attraction, everything you focus on, either negative or positive, will manifest.

Each time you ponder on your problems over and over you are hindering the process of the manifestation of dreams. When your mind wanders over your negative financial situation you cannot attract its opposite (abundance). In order to be more prosperous you should shift your thoughts and focus only on objects you desire. When you do so, keep your undivided attention on your desires all the time. You will always receive the same type of energy that you focus on.

Lastly a very important factor to manifest your desires is secretiveness. If your wishes have not been manifested yet, you should keep them secret. Their anticipated disclosure generally hampers their manifestation. Being secretive is a way to protect the manifestation of your dreams. You should always protect the things you desire, not commenting on them until they materialise. When you are secretive about your wishes you are less likely to be influenced by other people, especially negative persons.

For this reason it is important to avoid conversations about your desires with people who do not understand the Law of Attraction. If you talk to them about your wishes, they may make discouraging or disheartening remarks. Those comments, apparently innocent, may weaken your confidence in the manifesting process. Some of them may even make you doubt your dreams, undermining the whole process of manifestation. You may be influenced by their negative energy. For this reason, whenever possible you should keep your desires secret. Keep your desires protected from negative social conditioning.

# Section II

# Strategies to Manifest More Money

*Man's right to life means his right to have the free and unrestricted use of all the things which may be necessary to his fullest mental, spiritual, and physical unfoldment; or in other words, his right to be rich.*
*Wallace Wattles*

In this section we will explain a series of strategies to manifest money in an effortless manner. This toolbox will help you develop the conditions necessary to attract more prosperity into your life. In order to apply these tools it is important to have the mindset described in the previous section.

# Chapter 3

# Visualisation

*We live in a sea of plastic mind substance. The substance is ever alive and active. It is sensitive to the highest degree. It takes form according to mental demand. Thoughts form the mold or matrix from which the substance expresses.*
*Charles Haanel*

## 1. Subconscious and conscious mind

*Thoughts are seeds in the creative soil of mind.*
*Frederick Bailes*

It's important to explain the two main aspects of your mind and their functions. From the metaphysical perspective, your mind is divided into two aspects:

Subconscious mind
Conscious mind

### 1.1. Subconscious mind

*Your imagination is greater in its scope than you might think. It is the closest link to your soul. It is not bound by your past programmes, beliefs and fears. Imagination was given to you so you could transcend your physical world. It can create unlimited future pathways for you and help you look at the possible outcomes of various choices.*
*Roman Sanaya and Duane Packer*

This mind is also called the subjective mind. This mind is infinitely resourceful. It has unlimited wisdom and almighty power. This mind is unlimited, timeless and omniscient.

The subconscious does not differentiate real things from imaginary ones. You can affect it by using affirmations (a technique explained later in this book) or visualisations. It is easily affected by repeated suggestions. It is also impressed by vivid imagery. This is the creative part of your mind.

Your subconscious mind is still, non-linear, literal and receptive to new ideas. It isn't judgemental, rational or analytical. On the contrary, the subconscious trusts the conscious mind completely and does not argue with it. The subconscious mind never resists the messages of the conscious mind. Your subconscious always obeys the orders from your conscious. The subconscious mind does not recognise negative statements, for example if you say *"I don't want to be poor"*, the subconscious mind will understand "I want to be poor". It accepts any sentence as positive, even the grammatically negative ones.

The subconscious is also the storehouse of all your emotions and memories. It contains your long-term memory and is in charge of your automatic corporal functions. This part of your mind never rests; it is always working. Moreover it's moved by urges and aspirations. Your subconscious is the seat of your habits. It also manages your virtuous and automated activities. It is the source of intuition and fountain of your inspiration. It is the source of ideals and values.

Your subconscious level is the limitless part of your mind. It's all-powerful; it can do whatever you ask for. It's only constrained by the beliefs that you hold. It is also connected to the almighty universal forces. Your subconscious will find the easiest and the least resistant way to bring about what you desire. The subconscious obediently creates what you ask for, either good or bad.

## 1.2. Conscious mind

The conscious mind is also called the objective or superficial mind. It is related to short term-memory and it can grasp only a few pieces of information at once. This part of the mind receives impressions throughout five senses, in interaction with the subconscious mind. The conscious mind is the gatekeeper of the messages you receive from your environment. Your conscious is the conveyor of those messages to your subconscious.

Your conscious mind is your main resource when you use your willpower. The conscious level is rational, judgemental, analytical and problem-solving. It's the part of your mind involved in any decision-making process. The conscious mind deals with images, words and facts before they are imprinted on the subconscious mind.

## 2. Meaning of visualisation

*Visualization is simply the creation of strong mental images of the things desired, perfecting it each day until it becomes as clear as an existing material thing. Then the visualisation tends to materialise itself – that is, begins to build around itself actual material conditions corresponding with the mental framework.*
*William Walker Atkinson*

Visualisation is natural to you. Your mind naturally works with pictures so this technique is, in fact, an innate ability of yours. Visualisation is one of the quickest ways to manifest your wishes by design. If you apply this technique consistently, your desires will come to fruition when you least expect them.

Visualisation means having a vivid and compelling image in your mind about the objects of your desire. The images you have in mind can be accompanied with sounds, scents or tactile sensations to make them appear as real as possible.

For example you can visualise your bank statement having a balance of £1,000,000 or visualise yourself being paid that amount of money. You can imagine yourself counting the money and feeling the texture of the notes on your fingertips. You can also envision a phone call to confirm that you have that money in your account.

It's very important to know that when you are visualising you are using *your mind* to fabricate images. When you visualise *you are not using your sight*. When you visualise you are only using your imaginary inner forces, not your senses.

Visualisation is an essential transformative power within you. It's true that you always visualise naturally and spontaneously, sometimes focusing on negative things. For example, when you fear something, you are likely to visualise negative outcomes for a given situation.

A very important caveat is that you should only envision what you desire. You should never imagine getting rid of what you don't want, because, if you do so, you will be attracting the same undesired things. Your mind only attracts things, it doesn't repel anything.

Each time you visualise you use your thoughts. All thoughts have a specific vibration, either good or bad. When you hold positive images in your mind, you are radiating positive vibrations and, in turn, drawing back to you good things. Nevertheless when you hold negative images, you broadcast negative vibrations and consequently you will attract negative things to your life.

In order to make the vision more real you can imagine that your inner dialogue is positive, as if you had achieved your goal. For example, if you hold images of yourself having more money, you can accompany with statements such as *"I am prosperous"*, *"I am a rich person"*, among others. You can also imagine the positive comments or praise from other people because you have met your expectations.

When you visualise the objects of your desire, it is also important to feel that you are connected with the universal forces. Feel confident in the boundless universal supply which will satisfy all your desires in the best way.

Each time you visualise you are not a leaf flittering in the air blown by the capricious wind of uncontrolled circumstances. Instead, you are the captain of the ship which takes you to the best destinations. You are the designer of all your circumstances according to your most heartfelt desires.

You do not have to use visualisation to manipulate other people or exert any mental force over them. The visualisation tool is totally ineffective when you use it to manipulate others. In that sense, visualisation is useless when you try to make people act against their freewill. It is important not to project your images on your environment. Keep the images in your mind centred on you.

When you visualise you assert your claim about your desires. Each time you visualise you build up an accumulative effect to appropriate those desired objects.

All visualisation exercises are very useful to shape your belief system. This tool helps you replace outdated beliefs (e.g. scarcity) for new ones (for example, prosperity). In fact, each time you visualise you imprint your subconscious mind with the images, creating long lasting changes.

Another important thing to highlight is that visualisation is an ongoing process. In fact you are always manifesting what you visualised before, either recently or a long time ago. You may have visualised your current circumstances either consciously or unwittingly. To put it short, your current situation is the remainder of your past imaging.

The visualisation technique helps you fulfil your dreams, but also betters your attention span. Visualising on a frequent basis enhances your memory and creative skills. With continual practice you will notice those positive effects.

## 3. Characteristics of the visualisation process

*There is one original formless stuff, or substance from which all things are made... and which... permeates, penetrates and fills the interspaces of the universe... Man can form things in his thought, and, by impressing his thought upon formless substance, can cause the thing he thinks about to be created.*
*Wallace Wattles*

### A. Quality of images

When you visualise you should imagine yourself integrated in the images, being one with them. Your must see yourself inside your body when you envision your desires. Integration means that you look through your eyes at the desired objects or situations. According to Neuro Linguistic Programming, this method is called associate or integrative visioning.

So you should always see yourself as the main participant in the pictures you visualise. You are the most special protagonist acting in those imagined scenes. You have to avoid seeing yourself from outside, like an external observer (this method is called dissociate).

When you visualise try not to be too sensible with your imagination. You should always go beyond your comfort zone; you don't have to imagine "what is possible". Those images must be big, vivid and boundless.

Try to imagine yourself with things or events that you truly desire but you don't have now. It does not matter that what you visualise seems impossible to achieve right now. Trust the process and believe in yourself, and consequently you will see your desires materialised.

It's important to pinpoint that all images must be bright, colourful and bold. You can also use images sprinkled with glitter to make them more vivid. This will bring your desires forward more quickly. It is important for you to avoid dimmed or blurred images.

When you visualise you should use all your sensory impressions to shape the universal substance. If you use sounds they must be clear, the tactile sensations that you imagine must be lifelike.

In order to improve in the practice of visualisation, you can look at any trivial object, for example a table. Stare at the object for some seconds trying to grasp every detail. After this, try to create its image in your mind with your eyes closed. Then open your eyes and compare your images with the real object.

The use of images helps you build a familiarity bond with the objects of your desires. When you visualise, it is important that you also feel like owning or utilizing the desired things.

The object of your desired can also be visualised in a symbolic manner (for example, the £ sign). You must always use the most adequate symbols that correspond to your desires.

It is important to remember that the images you form in your mind should always be related to what you want, not to what you don't want. A very well known saying goes *"visualisation is like selecting a station in a radio"*. That means that, when you visualise, your desired objects you are broadcasting energy that draws them towards you.

So if you want to receive money you should be visualising yourself having more of it. Following this example, you cannot manifest money if you are visualising lack of it.

## B. Undivided attention

You should use your imagination, or capability of creating images, actively. You must be sternly engrossed in the imagery of your dreams. You must feel that you are completely involved in the process of visualisation. When you visualise your attention should not be fragmented during the process. Your focus must be clear and steady and your concentration intense and relaxed. This is the most effective way to embed the images in your subconscious and consequently manifest your dreams.

In order to visualise effectively, you must have a laser-like focus on the images you create. This means that your attention should not be distracted by any alien thought. Concentration and relaxation are two of the most important requirements for successful manifestation of your desires. You should never use the visualisation technique worriedly or forcefully.

Emmet Fox highlights that visualisation is like taking a photograph with a camera; you do this effortlessly. In that sense, you should focus on the images in your mind steadily, but at the same time smoothly. You should never scatter your attention over many different images. Just concentrate on the object of your desire in order not to dissipate your thoughts.

When you focus your attention on the image in your mind in an undivided manner you are less likely to be distracted by any other sensorial interference such as noise. Your mind must be placed on those images selectively and intently; you must shut it down to anything else.

It is also important that when you visualise you keep your mindset in alignment with the principles explained in the second chapter of this book (faith, positive emotions, idea of abundance, etc.). By abiding by those rules you will gradually strengthen your belief in the unlimited universal provision.

Some teachers say that when you visualise you should touch the area between your eyebrows with your finger. This is the third eye chakra and it is in charge of all the processes of visualisation. You can also imagine that your mind is a cinema projector which plays a movie that includes the desired objects or events.

Other teachers recommend, instead, that you should focus on your heart area when you visualise. When you do so, you should imagine love feelings going out from that region that tie you with the object of your desire.

It's important to know that sometimes the visualisation

process can be ineffective. Some of the reasons for this are: trying to visualise many things at the same time, tiredness, insufficient relaxation, distractions (noise, etc), or lack of focus on a specific outcome.

When you experience circumstances that are negative (for example, shortage of money) try to soften your attention on those undesired events. Instead, visualise the desired outcome (for example, having more money). Your focus should primarily be on the objects of your desire. You should be indifferent or detached from your current situation. This point will be analysed in detail below.

### C. Indifference before external circumstances

In fact, when you visualise you pay peripheral attention to your current reality (what it is). Instead, by using strong images, you concentrate on the desired conditions (what it is to be), which will manifest later consequently.

In this sense, when you visualise you do not submit yourself to external negative circumstances. You should have a strong belief that you cannot be defeated by those outward conditions because your essence is limitless. In fact, you calmly refuse to accept any negative current situation.

It was explained that any detrimental condition in your life is just a natural effect of the thoughts (causes) generated by your mind. For this reason, when you change your thoughts through visualisation, you are bound to transform your circumstances in the future. By thinking in a different way, you bring about new things into existence; your circumstances will change.

An example will clarify this point. If you have negative economic conditions, for example: you currently have very little money, then don't pay close attention to this situation. Instead, create images of prosperity in your mind. For example, you can imagine yourself receiving a big cheque. You can also visualise that your bank account has a millionaire's balance.

Besides, you can consider your current negative conditions as a starting point to be more effective with the visualisation process. To put this simply, when you practice visualisation you can use your present negative situation (for example, lack of money) as a means to reach a better condition. In this example, you take into account your current negative situation (insufficient money) and then visualise the opposite (for example, having a lot of money). You must hold this new vision steadfastly and your dire situation will improve naturally.

The visualisation technique is related to Robbins' advice. He says that you should always focus on the solution (your desired situation) and not on the problem (your current situation). Always shift your attention from things or events you do not desire, such as your current negative circumstances. Instead, only focus on what you can control, that is to say your thoughts and actions. By visualising regularly, the solutions to your problems will become clearer.

In conclusion, when you visualise, you always see things in the right manner. You are wilful to see what is true (for example, abundance, prosperity, etc.). By visualising you are not taken over by appearances (scarcity, lack, etc.). In this sense, Haanel said *"The creative thought is dominated by an ideal; the passive thought is dominated by appearances"*.

## D. Emotionalised

When you use visualisation the images must always be emotionalised. Your emotions give life to your vision. In this sense, Atkinson says that *"thoughts are cold, but feelings are warm, alive and vital"*; *"a feeling is a living thought"*.

By experiencing positive feelings when you visualise your dreams you speed up the whole manifestation process. Try to feel those emotions intensely pervading the area that goes from your neck to your crotch. The purest feelings to be used are joy, passion, acceptance, love and gratitude.

Each time you feel good you are vibrating positively. This is the most effective way to communicate your desire to the universal forces. The Universe will always send you something that matches your vibrations.

However you also have to be careful that you may inadvertently be sending the opposite vibrations regarding your most cherished desires. This happens when you experience, for example, fear, desperation, disappointment, self-pity, vacillation or neediness.

It was commented in this book before that fear and doubt make the manifestation process lose its momentum. In some cases, intense negative emotions can push your desired things faraway. For this reason, when you visualise, your thoughts should always be aligned with your emotions. There should not be any contradiction between both. In that respect, Jerry and Esther Hicks say *"you must find a way of feeling the excitement or satisfaction of your currently unrealized dreams before those dreams come to your reality"*.

If it is difficult for you to emotionalise your images positively, you can do a very simple exercise. Before visualising, try to remember some moments when you experienced good feelings in the past. For example, if you want to visualise much more money in your life, before doing so, you can remember past experiences when you felt prosperous (for example, times when you received a cheque or notes from someone). By recalling those experiences, you will evoke the past good feelings associated to them. So then you can link those emotions to the images of your dreams.

In accordance to this, Murphy states *"All that is necessary to express happiness and prosperity is to feel happy and prosperous "*. You must realise that underneath all your desires (such as having more money, buying a house or a car, etc.) there is only an essential one: experiencing positive emotions, being happy.

## E. Positive specific purpose

You can use visualisation for several purposes. In that sense, you can visualise yourself having more money, improving your appearance, being healthier, eliminating bad habits or having a good relationship, among other reasons.

When you visualise, it is helpful to know the needs you want to satisfy with the objects of your desire. For example, if you want to have £1,000,000 in your bank account, you should ask yourself *"Why do I want this money?"* or *"What are the needs this money can satisfy?"* Some examples of needs are security, self-worth, confidence, independence, etc.

Just by knowing the reasons why you want to have your dreams fulfilled, you will be in a more positive mood. In this way, you will radiate high vibrations, which in turn, will benefit and magnetise the whole visualisation process.

You can also use another strategy. Once you discover the underlying needs you can recall a situation in the past in which the same needs were satisfied. Relive that past memory for a while in order to evoke those positive feelings. Then refocus on the object of your desire. In this way you are linking those past emotions with your images.

It's important to know that each time you follow your heart-felt desires and visualise them the universal forces will support you unconditionally. The Universe is your best servant. The universal forces are your most loyal employees when you follow your dreams.

## F. Persistent relaxed attitude

It's important to be persistent with the images you visualise. However this does not mean that you should be obsessive, desperate or restless. Instead, you should be disciplined; you must practice visualisation every day if possible.

Persistence also means that you should stick to the images for a while for your desires to materialise. Every day give your dominant attention to the images in your mind for some minutes.

Each time that you visualise you will get more skilful at this technique. When you visualise on a frequent basis, you will become more aware of the invincible and unbounded creative power that provides you with everything.

When you visualise your dreams you are sending positive signals to the universe. Because of the law of causation, which states that every cause has an effect and every action has a reaction, you will certainly receive the objects or situation corresponding to your imagery.

Another important factor for successful visualisations is relaxation. Once you have visualised the objects of your desire you should carry on with your life in a relaxed manner. This means that you don't fret or worry about your desires at all. Instead, you do your activities and chores and rest assured that the universal forces will choose the right way for your dreams to manifest.

As we said before, things can be delayed in their manifestation. So if big or high priority things do not come to your life yet, you can visualise smaller ones. Your smaller desires are likely to materialise more easily while you wait for the big ones to come.

In conclusion, always bear in mind that you do not need to get tense when you visualise or even after this process. You must realise that materialisation of your wishes is always effortless, with no struggle. If you implement the visualisation technique this way rest assured that your dreams will unfold naturally

## G. State of allowance

When you ask the Universe for your desires you should be in a state of allowance. This state means not offering any resistance to the things about to come. In order to be receptive the quality of your emotions should be consistent with the manifestation process. You cannot manifest positive things (such as prosperity, love) if you are experiencing negative feelings (for example, anger or sadness).

For this reason, the visualisation process must be accompanied by empowering and energising feelings. The depictions in your mind should only be supported by good emotions, such as joyfulness, happiness, enthusiasm, calm anticipation, among others

On the contrary, you are actually resisting the materialisation of your desires when you experience hesitation, doubt, fear or anxiety. When you visualise you also should leave aside other negatives states such as unworthiness, restlessness or impatience.

For example, when you fear something you tend to visualise negative outcomes, the ones that you are scared about. In order to counteract this, you must take back control of your images. You should deliberately visualise positive end results.

All negative emotional states create resistance. Those feelings are obstacles to the manifestation of your dreams. That is because you radiate vibrating patterns that are totally incompatible with the materialisation of your wishes. As a matter of fact, your negative feelings hinder the visualisation process.

If you notice any resistance, you can also imagine that you are bathing it in white or violet light. Envision the ray of light dissolving all opposition.

## H. Transmuting power

When you visualise your ideas you actually imprint the physical world with your thoughts in order to shape it according to your wishes. With your visualisations you are like a sculptor working with clay; you purposefully knead and mould the spiritual universal energy to bring about your dreams.

You must realise that you are the only creator of all things about to come into your life. You should know that the Universe is always on your side and you should rely on its forces unreservedly. By visualising you are consciously channelling the universal immaterial energy to manifest your desires.

The visualisation technique allows you to shape the external circumstances according to your thoughts with unerring precision. If you use the visualisation technique frequently you will also strengthen your trust in the universal forces.

Visualisation implies a process of transmutation. By visualising you actually bring the metaphysical immaterial substance into the physical material world. You turn the non-manifested into manifested. You transform the limitless, shapeless and timeless matter into things limited in space and form. Each time you visualise you turn the universal energy into specific things.

When you use this tool regularly, you will become more cognizant of your innate dominion over reality. You will realise that, as some sages say, you are a midwife of the universal energy, capable of bringing about any definite form you desire.

## I. Positive expectancy

Visualisation is a useful and simple technique with far-reaching effects. When you visualise, you should always surrender to the forces of the universe. You should truly believe you deserve the objects of desire.

You must feel that your wishes will manifest in your life. In the depth of your heart, you must know that the Universe is generous and boundless. When using the visualisation technique you should never position yourself in a place of lack. On the contrary, have consciousness of abundance.

Visualisation is a very powerful technique. By visualising you go beyond your current negative circumstances, you are connecting with the future throughout your visions. For this reason, you must positively expect in relation to the manifestation of your desires. In that effect, there should not be any doubt or conflicting thinking regarding the materialisation of your wishes.

Faith and peacefulness are states that contribute to attract your desired situation into your life. You must be confident that the Universe will answer your request.

There is a very important caveat to highlight. In the beginning it is very unlikely that your desires will manifest instantaneously, they will take some time to turn up. You have to understand that the universal forces have their own timing, the ideal one. So any delay in the materialisation of your desires does not mean denial from the Universe.

## J. Detachment from the outcome

When you practice visualisation, you should have an attitude of detachment from three different perspectives. In that sense, you should be detached from:

the results of the process
your current circumstances
specific ways that your desires will materialise

First of all, you must be detached from the results of the visualisation process. This means that, if the objects of your desire do not materialise, you can continue with your life unworriedly. You realise that you can be happy regardless of the manifestation of your wishes. When you have this attitude you will never feel miserable if the objects don't manifest. It seems counterintuitive but, when you are unworried about results, your desires tend to materialise more quickly.

Secondly, you should be detached from your current situation. This means that you don't have to pay close attention to your current negative circumstances. Your mind is to be focused only on positive imagery.

Thirdly you do not make any assumptions about how the universe will manifest your dreams. The way your desires will be materialised are under the control of the universal forces. You don't have to draw any conclusion in advance about how your desires will be fulfilled.

In fact, you only have to envision the end results, but not their way of materialising. Let the Universe choose the means through which your wishes will come true. By having a detached attitude regarding the ways your desires will manifest, you are open to the unbounded creativity of the universal forces. In this way you become receptive to any of the innumerable ways the Universe selects to make your dreams true.

When you try to select a way for your dreams to be manifested you are trying to outpace universal forces. This attitude will hinder the overall manifestation process. So always give up any control over the means or timing of the manifestation process. The Universe is the only one in charge of that.

To summarise this, you don't have to visualise how you will get the desired things, only envision the end results. Remember the means for the materialisation of your desires is always a domain of universal forces.

## K. Rehearsal

*I wake up in the morning and I consciously create my day the way I want it to happen... now sometimes because my mind is examining all the things that I need to get done, it takes me a little bit to settle down and get to the point of where I am... intentionally creating my day... When I create my day and out of nowhere little things happen that are so unexplainable, I know that they are... the result of my creation and the more I do that, the more I build a neuron net in my brain that I accept that that's possible, it gives me the power and the incentive to do it the next day.*

*Dr. Joe Dispense (from the movie "What the bleep do we know!?")*

Whether your realised this or not, when you visualise you are in a state of "as if". You imagine as if you had certain things. You see yourself having those things and feel in possession of them.

In your mind you own the desired object. You should act as if the object of your desire had materialised. In that effect, visualisation is a way of rehearsing your desires before they turn up.

And the Universe always finds the best way to bridge the distance between the rehearsed ideal images (your desired objects) and your current situation (lack of those objects). The almighty provision will bring your desires into manifestation.

You can pose some questions to rehearse future scenarios in your life. In order to have a more effective visualisation you can ask yourself *"What if..?"* or *"How would it be if...?"* A specific example for this is *"How would it be if I had £1,000,000 in my bank account?"* This type of question prompts you to create specific images in your mind. In fact, you are rehearsing mentally some possible scenario to find the answer. And when you are looking for the answer you are simply visualising.

Another useful question to use is *"Wouldn't it be nice to have...?"* Other questions that can help you with the visualisation process are *"Why do I want this?"* and *"What are the main details of this?"* All of them will help you to visualise more effortlessly.

## L. Internal process

Visualisation is an inward process. In that sense, Haanel states that *"affluence within results in affluence without"*. This means that what you see without is a literal expression of your world within. For this reason, your internal world must be balanced if you want to produce positive outcomes in your life. Your thoughts must be positive if you want to attract positive circumstances. So in order to have a harmonious inner world, you must be capable of controlling your thoughts and emotions, and keeping them positive.

Visualisation is always a within-out inventive process. You hold images in your mind, or your internal world, and then they materialise in your external world, or your life circumstances. It's not a process outside-in; in this second case you see your circumstances, which is your external world, and believe in them, making them part of your internal world.

To put this simply, all the images that you visualise and impress internally (on your subconscious mind) will later express outwardly (in your environment, as materialised things). When you materialise your desires you actually turn the unseen into seen.

By now you must be aware that your thoughts have limitless creative power. In that sense, your thoughts are actions in progress. Your thinking is the cause of your current life situation, not its consequence. Your reality, as you perceive it, is the natural consequence of your thoughts.

For this reason, you should not be working on your current negative circumstances to sort them out. Instead, work on your thoughts, change your thoughts and your life situation will change. You will unerringly attract what you dwell upon on a continual basis. So it is useless to work on the conditions. You should rather work on your thoughts, transform them into positive ones.

In conclusion, you are the only creator of your life conditions. For this reason, you should never react to external circumstances; you can solely change them by changing your thoughts.

## M. Mental equivalent

Emmet Fox says that everything you have in your life has a mental equivalent. According to this perspective, for new things to appear in your life you must edify their mental equivalents. The mental equivalent is a solid and clear image of what you want. When you create the image of the desired object you should feel in possession of it. So if you want to have more money in your life, you have to depict the mental equivalent of this. As time goes by, the desired money will turn up in your life.

On the other side, you must also eliminate the equivalents of what is undesired. For example, if you don't want to be poor any longer, you must destroy the mental images of this. When you destroy those images, your economic situation will improve drastically.

The visualisation process is a good tool to mentally construct those mental equivalents. On one side, you should only visualise what you want. On the other side, you must eliminate any image of what is unwanted. In this way you substitute negative equivalents by positive ones, your circumstances will change accordingly.

You design a mental equivalent of your desires when you think about them in a continual, clear and heartfelt manner. In that effect the successful manifestation process is always a combination of intended thinking with intense emotion.

It is advisable to maintain your focus on the good equivalent without going back to the negative one, at least for a month. In relation to prosperity, for example, you can imagine that the balance in your bank account is £1,000,000 without paying attention to the actual current balance of £1,000.

From this perspective, you should think, act and talk as if the old equivalent (in the previous example, your little bank account balance) never existed. Only focus on the object of your desire, hold the positive equivalent in your mind (in the example, the imagined bank account balance of £1,000,000).

In conclusion, each thing that is in your life, either positive or negative, has a mental equivalent. Negative things cannot disappear unless you dissolve or substitute their mental equivalents.

## N. Inspired action

When you visualise your desires, this does not mean that you have to take immediate action regarding them. In that sense, you should never be overacting or acting impulsively to achieve your dreams.

You must realise that you cannot force the manifestation of

your desires throughout your actions. On the contrary, each time you take desperate actions, you are actually hampering the materialisation of your desires.

For this reason, in relation to your wishes, you should only take inspired actions. You should only act in accordance to your inner guidance. This means that you should only act when you feel that it is appropriate, you should never act just because you have to.

All inspired actions tend to be effortless. When you act in an inspired manner, you generally spend a minimum amount of energy and things seem to flow spontaneously. In that sense, Pauley and Pauley say that *"individual accomplishment is an overrated value. In truth, we do not earn, achieve, accomplish or attain anything except by the grace of the Universe"*. It is important that, when you see some signals or clues in relation to the objects of your desire, you take inspired action, if necessary. From the metaphysical perspective, it is not working hard, but taking inspired heartfelt action which makes things progress in your life.

## O. Other aspects

It has been set out that visualisation entails the use of your intellectual and emotional resources to achieve goals. However, it is important to pinpoint that all those resources are to be used at present. This means that all visualisation exercises are carried out in the now. In that effect, the present moment is your only moment of power to visualise. You can change your current conditions, visualising the future ones now. Imagine your future beneficial situations as if they were real right now.

Another important point to highlight is that your imaginative thinking (creating ideal images of the future) is many times more powerful and expansive than your rational thinking (that is analysing your current circumstances). Inventive thinking is more potent because when you create something new, you are not tied to the past. When you envision, you are not constrained by your belief system, which is very restrictive.

Lastly, here are some more tips to make your visualisation process more effective. You can include positive affirmations related to the objects you are visualising. Some good examples of affirmations are *"I am delighted because... I enjoy...."* In this way you are guiding the visualisation process with your words.

You can also state that you want the objects to be manifested in total harmony with all people involved. Besides this, you can visualise thinking or saying *"I have permission to receive this or something better"*. When you say that, feel worthy of receiving the things you visualise.

## 4. Techniques of visualisation

*Manifestation through creative visualization is the process of realizing and making visible on the physical plane our divine potential.*
*Shakti Gawain*

### 4.1. Images of opulence

There is an interesting technique to visualise a prosperous life. You can imagine improving your finances. You must see yourself in a wealthy position. You should envision yourself on a specific future date on which you would have become affluent. Imagine that you are rich. See yourself having everything that you desire, cars, houses, and other properties. Imagine having all the experiences of your ideal life. Dwell on those images, feel the related sensations, sounds and emotions.

Then imagine yourself in an even wealthier position one year later. See how you will feel at that time and act. Visualise an even more prosperous position five and ten years later. After all those images, imagine your wealth energy pervading your body and everything around you. You will feel more energised after this exercise.

Some authors like McKenna recommend that you should see yourself having had money at different early ages. That means that you imagine how your life would have been at different past stages of your life, if you had had plenteous money and all your economic needs met. For example, you can imagine a prospering childhood, a wealthier adolescence and an even more affluent adulthood. You must imagine yourself having all your financial expectations fulfilled at all your past ages. This technique will reprogramme your mind to receive more abundance.

A very simple technique is visualising physical evidences that you are in a thriving financial situation. In that effect, you can visualise that your bank statement has bigger balances. You can see yourself holding big stacks of money. You can also imagine spending those notes on the objects of your desire. You can envision your salary slips with higher wages. Try to hold clean-cut images during this exercise.

Some masters state that, instead of visualising a certain amount of money, you should envision the specific things you want to buy with it. For example, you can imagine purchasing a flat, a car or a computer. In some cases, you can see a specific situation such as the signing of a contract to buy an apartment.

You can also use this visualisation technique while you listen to some calming music. Try to choose songs with positive lyrics and soothing melodies. The use of this type of music will help you intensify your good emotions and clarify your visions.

When you carry out your daily tasks, you should only entertain your mind with images of opulence. Look at any conflicting image that appears in your mind and fade it away immediately. During the day, try to be consistent with your positive thoughts about abundance. Evoke prosperity images again and again and feel connected with the universal stream of affluence.

Avoid thinking too much about your negative financial conditions. This can actually be very tricky because those external circumstances may look so "real". Most people fervently believe in their negative external situations and act accordingly. Instead, don't pay attention to your negative circumstances. Hold your ideal images about affluence tight to your mind.

It was said before that you should imagine yourself having a lot of money. Besides this, you can also visualise yourself living in an abundant world. In this world all people are becoming more prosperous and they have all their needs and dreams fulfilled. That means that you must imagine rich people becoming even richer and poor people becoming wealthier. This technique will help you eliminate any resentment toward people that are currently rich. When you visualise this, imagine yourself radiating positive energy of love to the planet.

## 4.2. Vision board

There is a very well known technique used for visualisation called vision board or treasure map. In order to use this tool, you can use magazines and newspapers and cut out some pictures from them. You must only select photographs that represent the objects of your desire. Then you have to glue the pictures on a carton board to make a poster or a collage with them.

Once the vision board is made, look at this board frequently. When you do so, imagine vividly being in possession of the objects or living those events, in both cases related to the pictures stuck on the board. Your vision must include as many senses as possible, such as touch, smell, sight, etc. You should repeat this exercise as much as you like, at least once a day. You should have positive expectancy as if your desires have already been manifested. Also be grateful for the generous provision from the Universe.

The board acts as a physical prop for the visualisation of your desires, like a reminder of your dreams. It is a facilitator that assists you during the visualisation process.

The vision board can be a poster, but also a scrapbook. You may prefer to have your mini vision board in a notepad because it is portable and you can take it with you wherever you go. You can also design your vision board and store it in a file on your computer or mobile.

The vision board can include, besides the pictures, drawings and affirmations. You can make one vision board for each of your goals or a general one for all of them. You can also include glitter and any other adornment to make the vision board more visually enticing.

Instead of having a vision board you can use a dream box. In that box put all the articles, pictures, drawings and affirmations related to the objects of your desire. It's important to have a look at the content of that box on a frequent basis.

## 4.3. Images or movies

You can visualise still images related to the objects or situations of your dream, but you can also imagine a movie with them. In the latter case, you can imagine a film related to your desires in which you are the protagonist. For example, if you want to have more money, this mind movie should show scenes of you enjoying your prospering financial situation.

This movie can be played in your mind in slow or quick motion. The movie can be coloured or black and white, and with sound or soundless. You can use the same movie time and again, or you can replace it for a better one. It is important that the main scenes display your desires being fulfilled.

You should give emphasis to certain aspects of that mental film such as sensations, emotions, thoughts and other details. You can envision other characters in the movie that interact with you.

NLP (Neuro Linguistic Programming) suggests that you should be integrated to the movie. This means that you are looking at the scenes through your eyes, touching with your hands, and so on. You don't see your body from outside.

You can also write down a movie script of prosperity. In this script you must include your ideal financial situation for the next day, week, month or year. You can prepare this script at any time. You can also improve the script over time, adding more details to it. Then you should visualise the enacting of the content of the script engrossingly. Visualise the movie related to the film, making the images vivid and lively.

## 4.4. Beam of light

Denning and Philips give an interesting exercise to practise visualisation. You must visualise your desired object in front of you in a vivid manner. At the same time you must imagine a potent beam of light coming from the Universe. This light enters your body from the top of your head. You should see the ray filling your body.

Then you project this beam outside from your solar plexus. You must visualise that this beam of light envelopes the desired object. You should use that ray to magnetise the object envisioned.

These authors also include a technique called multiplication, For example, focus on a object that you want to be multiplied for example, money, put a note in front of you, envelope with the beam of light. At the same time feel the sensation of the multiplication of that object. After this, you can say to the Universe that this object is enough for you and that you own it cheerfully. You can also bless the object on behalf of the universal power. It's advisable to practice this exercise daily at the same time.

## 4.5. Use of visual aids

You can also use some physical props called visual aids. They will help you with the process of visualisation. An example of these props is the design fake cheques. You prepare the cheques manually or with your computer. Try to make the cheques similar to the original ones. A very obvious caveat is that the cheques will only be used for the purpose of visualisation.

The cheques should be issued as if they are to be collected by you. They must include the amount of money that you want to materialise. Once you have the cheques in hand, visualise them for a while every day. When you do so, feel as if they are real and you are entitled to cash them in.

Another example of this, similar to the previous one, is a fake bank statement. You can also prepare fake bank statements with the balance that you want to manifest. In some cases you can use the real bank statement and delete the actual balance and write the one you want to materialise. Also visualise this statement on a frequent basis. A third example is the use of a fake cash ledger. You have to record in the ledger the amount of money you want to turn up. Use these props for visualisation only.

Another visual aid that you can use is fake news. You can prepare this article with your computer. You can also make a collage from different news articles. In this article it appears that you fulfil your dreams, for example, you earn £1,000,000. Try to make the article as lifelike as possible, as if it were real news. In order to fabricate this article, you can take the format of articles from a newspaper or magazine that you like. Some examples of news to be used are "Mr... has a net worth of..." or "Mr... bought the mansion located at....", among others.

You can also use other physical props, for example you can keep real notes for an amount of £100 in your wallet or purse at all times. Then every time you go past a shop you must imagine yourself spending the notes on the things shown there that you want to buy. Do this many times in your imagination. You have only to visualise that you spend the notes. It's a mental rehearsal so you don't have to buy anything in practice.

By having a look at these visual aids frequently, you will find it easier to visualise and attract more money. With the used of these props, you will get more familiar with the experiences of receiving more money. You will evoke feelings related to abundance more easily.

## 4.6. River of abundance

Roberts suggest a very simple but powerful exercise. You should visualise a never ending river of abundance going into your left arm passing through your chest and going out from your right arm. After this, you must close your arms and feel the flow of prosperity all over your body.

There is another way of using this technique. You should imagine yourself swimming in a gold river. Feel the liquid gold soaking into your skin. You should imagine yourself relishing in the gold water. Feel your body completely impregnated by the gold substance.

## 4.7. List of desires

*Men draw toward themselves that which they Desire.*
*William Walker Atkinson*

You can also visualise that you write a list with all your desires. Imagine that this list is addressed to the Universe, which is the recipient. If you want to have more money, you must visualise that you write down this wish in a specific way. You can see yourself writing down on the list a certain amount of money, a car, a house, trips, clothes or any other thing of your desire.

After this, you imagine that you send the list to the universal forces. You see yourself delegate those dreams to the Universe. You should feel confident and reliant on the universal all-mighty power. During this process you should rest assured that the universal forces will manifest those desires.

## 4.8. Golden Images

Silva recommends a technique called "golden images". This

technique is used in a discipline called mind control. In order to use this tool you should enter a state of meditation to calm your thoughts. The different meditation techniques will be explained later in this book. When your mind is calm and your body relaxed, imagine your present negative circumstances. For example, your current conditions may be about lack of money. See those current circumstances clearly in your mind and frame that image in blue.

On the top left corner of the image you should see a small blurry image of the desired situation, for example, yourself having a lot of money. This desired image will be framed in white. You must count up to three and utter the word "change", and swap the images. The small image framed in white becomes big, and the big image framed in blue becomes small.

However the image framed in blue (now small) must appear in the bottom left corner of the big white image. That image must be blurred and out of focus. Instead the white image (now big) will have lively colours and enhanced details.

The purpose of this exercise is to replace your mental images of the undesired (lack of money) for the desired (abundance). You can repeat this exercise as many times as you want. When you practise this exercise in a relaxed and meditative state, the new image will imprint your subconscious mind, replacing the old one.

## 4.9. Flood of images

One interesting technique to mother and manifest your desires is the following one. You should flood your mind with vivid images of the objects or situations you want to manifest in your life. You should imagine that your mind is inundated by that imagery. You must feel as if your mind was a mental canvass pervaded by those images.

There is not a right or wrong way to do this exercise. Do it in the way you feel more comfortable. Beware of the intensity and vividness of the images that impregnate your mind. It is important that you use bold and lively pictures. You should accompany those images with positive vigorous feelings. You should also feel connected with the Universe. Feel in unity with the infinite infallible power.

## 4.10. Coil technique

This technique is suggested by Roman and Packer. They recommend that you should imagine yourself being a potent powerhouse generating positive energy. You should see yourself having a coil, with a shape of a hoop going around and around. See that coil situated on your solar plexus inside your body. See the coil expanding from that area and pervading your whole body with energy. See the coil also expanding outside with its energy.

Then you must visualise the object of your desire outside you. After this imagine that you draw the object towards you using the coil. So drag that object to you and place it in a specific part of your body, like your heart or throat. If this exercise is done correctly, once you placed the imagined object in your body, you will feel a sensation such as a click or the fading of energy.

## 4.11. Visions of forgiveness

You can also visualise forgiveness. In that case you can see yourself forgiving people that hurt you. You must also forgive yourself for all your past mistakes. In order to attract more money you can visualise yourself forgiving all the people that deceived you financially. As an example of this, you can see yourself forgiving all the people that had not paid their debts to you.

This exercise will help you to have good energy. When you forgive yourself or others you generate positive vibration. In that sense, this will make you more receptive to the manifestation of your desires, for example having more money in your life.

Besides, you can also imagine yourself sending love to the people you forgave. You can also imagine that, in turn, you receive multiplied loving energy from them. The love energy can be visualised as an intense pink or white ray coming from your heart.

## 4.12. Chamber in your heart

Some specialists such as Rebecca recommend a very interesting exercise to practise visualisation. You must visualise the object of desire from a certain distance. Then you should imagine in your heart area a small chamber with the exact shape of the object desired. Also imagine that this chamber has the same vibration as the object you desire.

You must visualise that from the chamber a beam of light goes out of your body and connects with the object. Then you should use the beam to reel the object into the chamber, fitting it in perfectly and effortlessly. At that moment you try to feel the joy of having manifested your desire.

## 4.13. Other techniques

**Future moods:** You can also imagine how your activities will be affected after the manifestation of your desires. Some questions that you can ask yourself in this process are *"How will my mood be when I manifest this?"* or *"How will my daily activities be affected after the materialisation of my desire?"*.

**Throwing worries away:** You can also imagine that you expel all your worries out from your mind. You can depict your worries as clouds. Then see them pushed out of your mind by a potent wind. Imagine those worries flying far away until they disappear from your sight.

**Energy ray:** You can also visualise rays going throughout your body. A ray that is commonly used is the violet flame. This ray is used to transmute negative energies, for example vibrations of scarcity. Another important ray you can use is the golden ray. This ray can be used to attract more prosperity to your life.

**Love light:** This technique can be used whenever you are walking down a street. You should visualise your way ahead covered with loving light. You imagine yourself surrounded by love pervading everything and everyone with loving energy. The love energy has a very high vibration. This energy will hasten the manifestation of all your desires, even having more money.

**Bubble:** It is interesting to highlight this technique suggested by Gawain. Every time you visualise an object, you must envelope it in a pink bubble. This bubble represents love. Then imagine that you release the bubble enclosing the desired object to the universe. See the bubble floating far away.

**Prosperity contract:** Another interesting exercise is to imagine that you sign a contract to be poor. The contract can say something like this: *"Mr... commits to be poor because of...."* Imagine that you sign the contract. Then see yourself destroying the agreement; tearing it in pieces. You can also stamp it with the text "cancel". After this, imagine that you sign a new contract. In this agreement you are committing to be rich. Imagine that this agreement is kept in a safe place. It is said that this type of exercise helps you replace your negative beliefs about money for positive ones.

# Chapter 4

# Generosity Attitude

## 1. Giving

*For our purposes it is really only necessary to recognize that power is that which makes you go strong, Force makes you go weak. Love, compassion and forgiveness which may by some be mistakenly thought of as submissive are, in fact, profoundly empowering. Revenge, judgmentalism and condemnation, on the other hand, inevitably make you go weak... Power attracts, whereas force repels.*
*David Hawkins*

### 1.1. The universe strikes balance

*The law of attraction says whatever you give, you receive... (it) is a mirror, an echo or boomerang or a copying machine.*
*Rhonda Byrne*

When you have read the title "generosity attitude", it is very likely that you have thought something like this: *"I want to receive more money, what the heck has giving to do with receiving more money?"* In relation to that, it's important to highlight that the universal laws don't work one way; instead, receiving money is always part of a flow, which includes giving and receiving. In that effect, if you only expect to receive money without making it circulate at all, your prosperity will not go further.

To put this simply, from the metaphysical viewpoint, when you give more, you will always receive more. The universal forces always tend to strike balance, throughout natural compensation. Everything in the Universe is in balance. In that sense, you cannot give without receiving; each time that you give, you will receive naturally. From the universe's perspective, everything has a very subtle but also precise equilibrium.

A good metaphor that is commonly used is the respiration process; you cannot only inspire (receive air), you should also expire (expel air) to live. Some say that what you give to others will come back to you multiplied. It's important to know that in most of the cases you will receive from other sources, different from the ones you originally gave to.

Every time you give, you are radiating positive vibrations. The generosity attitude always exudes positivity; it only brings you good things. Giving must be unconditional, with the only purpose to support others. When you are obliging with others, you show that you have a generous spirit. By assisting other people with their activities, you generate positive energy based on love and selflessness.

You don't have to give with the expectation to receive more. In fact you must not have any expectation of return, although it will naturally manifest. You should always give without any reservation. If not, that is not giving but bribing or bartering. If possible, try to give joyously, regularly and humbly. In that sense, your giving should be gracious and heart-felt. The term "giving" does not involve only money, but also other good things, such as love, peace, compliments, smiles, advice, among others.

There is an interesting sociological aspect of giving. Cialdini pinpoints that, because of the social principle of reciprocity, each time you give the receiver will feel indebted to you. In any case, the receiver will feel compelled to reciprocate your good actions. However, from the metaphysical perspective, you should give without any expectation to receive anything in exchange for your gifts. But rest assured that the Universe will reciprocate in the most unexpected ways for your presents.

## 1.2. Your attitude when you give

Some spiritual teachings say that the most important and gratifying drive of all human beings is to give love to others. When you give, you implicitly are also giving love. It is important that you give what you can to other people whenever possible. Some recommend to give something (either monetary or not), to at least three different people each day. Some examples are: giving compliments to a relative or friend, spare money to a beggar, unused clothes to a Charity or good wishes to someone. Every time you give, do it from a perspective of selflessness. As it was mentioned before, you should not be expecting anything from the person that receives your gifts.

Generosity should always be practised from a place of happiness and joy. On the contrary, you should never give anything from a place of anxiety or expectation of reciprocity. Moreover you should never give out of obligation or guilt. You don't have to brag about what you gave either; you don't have to give to show off. Giving never has to be felt as if you were sacrificing something. On the contrary, when you give, you should feel that you are sharing what you have with others in a loving and delightful manner. When you have a generosity attitude, you give liberally, not constrainedly.

Besides, each time you give, your own sense of worth will improve dramatically. You are likely to consider yourself more useful and of more value to people. You also experience more peace and vitality, just because of having given. You will realise the main aspects of your humanness, which might have been hidden by detrimental social conditioning. It is important to highlight that generosity is considered one of the most important factors to achieve success, from the financial perspective and others.

## 1.3. Your connection to others

Each time you give you recognise that you are connected to

others; you honour the underlying interconnection that links everything. In that sense, we are all connected to one another. All our good actions regarding others will have a positive impact on them, but also on ourselves. When you give selflessly, you realise your close kinship with other people. At the same time, every time you give positive things to others, you keep your vital energy circulating; you are not hoarding it. When your energy becomes stagnant, your vibration is contrary to the manifestation of good things in your life. For this reason, giving is always a natural attractor of prosperity and wealth in your life. You will notice that when you give more, the universal forces will give you back even more, through different and generally unexpected sources.

Besides, giving is a very important factor of a prosperity mindset. When you have a prosperous attitude, regardless of the amount of money or properties you have, you behave generously. This attitude implicitly tells the universe that you are so appreciative with all that you have that you don't mind sharing it with others. As a consequence of this, the universal forces will reward you with even more than what you give.

Each time you give you are also sending a message to your subconscious mind of deservedness. You are telling your subconscious that you can give because you don't see any scarcity in your life. In that sense, you imprint the idea that you believe that you are always entitled to receive good things from the universe. So for that reason you don't mind giving generously.

It is important to mention a very relevant caveat regarding giving. Everything that you give must be positive or for positive use, both in the case of material or intangible things. A very obvious example of when not to give, according to this perspective, is giving money to someone who, you know for sure, will spend it on drugs. In that example, there is no positive use in the object you gave. In that case, your generous attitude doesn't help the recipient at all.

## 1.4. Anything can be given

As it was mentioned before, giving is not only about material things, such as money or any other stuff. Giving also includes providing advice, knowledge, work, love, respect, good examples, time and caresses, among others. In some cases, such as giving good advice or precise technical knowledge, it is obvious that you can help others to improve their lives. However, in all cases when you give in a loving manner, your gifts have something remarkable for the recipients.

From the metaphysical viewpoint, helping others in a selfish and random manner is also called an "act of kindness". From this wider perspective, you decide to help strangers, only because you feel you should do so. In that sense, giving is not only limited to benefitting people that you know, anyone is deserving of your gift. So try to carry out these acts whenever possible, they will benefit others as well as you.

Each time you give money to other people do this from a perspective of abundance. This means that you should feel that you are getting more prosperous and the recipients too. You can also participate in altruistic or philanthropic activities. Charity, social service, donation, mentoring, child fostering, volunteering are different ways of giving. All these egoless activities, in which you have the role of a benefactor, have the positive aspects mentioned before.

Besides, don't forget to give to yourself regularly. Pamper yourself with little or big gifts, indulge in pleasurable activities frequently. Each time you do so, you are broadcasting signals to the universe of gratitude and joy. This will hasten the manifestation of your desires.

## 1.5. Giving in the entrepreneurial world

*The focus should be to provide the best service possible not on earning the maximum amount of money... Put the service first and money will take care of itself.*
*David Schwartz*

### Being generous as an employee

When you are working for a company as an employee or employer, you should also have a generosity attitude. In that sense, you should give your best to all people you deal with. When you work for an organisation as an employee, you should try to generously provide the company you work for with your services. Try to always have a loving attitude towards your employer.

When you are an employee, try to deliver equal value (or higher, if possible) in relation to your income. Consider that you are a very important factor offering your employer your unique skills; you are part of the interface between the inner world of the company (processes of production, selling, administration, etc.) and its environment (clients, competitors, suppliers, etc.).

Try to co-operate with other work mates whenever possible. Try also to work in groups, if possible, to complement your own skill in working with others. Team-playing has a synergic effect that results in higher value added to the company. There is an appendix at the end of the book that highlights the advantages of co-operation.

From the metaphysical perspective, always use your strengths and talents to serve the company you work for in the best way possible. Try to add value to your activities whenever possible. Consider your work as a part of your higher purpose, your mission in this life. Besides, try to put people first, by providing them with your best service. If you act this way you will certainly receive a higher compensation. If you don't like your current job, act in an obliging manner all the same. If you do so, the universal forces will naturally set you in the right post unexpectedly.

If you work, for example, in the sales department you must give the best advice to customers. Support all clients when you are selling them products or services. Don't confuse or deceive them with selling gimmicks. Instead, always provide them with the products and services that meet their needs properly. In that effect, you must always treat the clients as you would like to be treated if you were in their place.

### Being generous as an employer

In the case that you are an employer you should also have a giving attitude. In that sense, you must be generous to others, in relation to material or immaterial things. Always try to give your best to suppliers, workers, clients, etc. Switch your focus from maximising profits to providing your clients with the best services and products that satisfy, or even exceed, their needs.

Of course, you always have to obtain a reasonable amount of profit. However this will be the natural consequence of the application of the principles of giving. When you give your best value, profits are generated automatically, they take care of themselves.

When you give your clients more value, they are very likely to become loyal, and buy more from your company. For example, you can implement different strategies to provide higher value, such as free gifts, trial period for products, money-back guarantees, convenient financing, free delivery, training, etc. All these bonuses will certainly delight customers; you are likely to exceed their needs. With this attitude you don't have to worry about competitors, clients will come to you spontaneously; they will choose your products willingly.

From the prosperity perspective, think that you are only competing with yourself, and not with other companies, as you might have believed in the past. For this reason, you provide with a much higher value than before. When your company gives, that means by providing excellent services and valuable goods, you will effortlessly bring about more profits.

Most of the companies are focused on the opposite; they try to obtain (receive) money from clients, instead of focusing on giving, which will, in turn, generate more receiving or income. When your company is purposefully adding meaningful value to clients, they will give you their money effortlessly.

The same principle applies to your employees and other stakeholders. Your stakeholders are all the people or organisations with interest in your organisation, such as suppliers, banks, community, partners, employees, etc. For example, in the case of employees, treat them with respect and motivation. Reward them fairly for the work they provide to your company. The same perspective must be applied to other stakeholders. In the case of competitors, consider developing co-operative alliances with them. There is an appendix that explains the main implications of co-operation at the end of this book.

You should identify the main stakeholders of your company and contribute to their lives significantly, directly and indirectly. Allen says that true service is *"to forget oneself in love towards all, to lose oneself in working for the whole"*

## Tithe

> *Tithing is not an end but a means towards the end of totally living in a giving consciousness.*
> *Eric Butterworth*

Tithe is another way of giving with positive effects on your life. In that effect, tithing is the basis for your financial success. When you tithe you give part of your money to a church or any other social bodies such as foundations, schools, charities, associations, etc. You are the one who decides the recipient of this amount of money. Try to choose the one or ones you feel contribute to spiritual progress.

Tithing is a very significant way of detachment. From the metaphysical perspective, when you tithe, you are returning to the Universe part of the money that you have. You should always tithe out of love; tithe actively and joyously. You should never tithe because you feel obliged. Instead you should tithe because you want to share your resources with others.

Some say that you should tithe ten per cent of your income. So in this case tithing is proportional to the level of your prosperity; when you have more money you will tithe more. However others say that you should tithe whatever you feel able to give. The most important thing, regardless of the amount that you tithe, is that you can give unreservedly and fearlessly.

When you tithe you should have a supportive and loving attitude. The act of tithing should never feel mandatory; on the contrary, it should be a spontaneous action. Each time you tithe, you are implicitly asserting to the Universe (or God) that all your basic needs are satisfied, and that you are grateful for this.

It is said that when you tithe, you just give what you owe to the universal forces because of being on this planet. It's like the rent that you pay for living on Earth. According to this perspective, you should always give unconditionally because the resources you own are not actually yours; you are the Universe's resources manager.

Some authors such as Speller state that what you tithe will bring you a tenfold return. According to this perspective each time that you give money to a social helpful organisation such as a hospital, school, or a church you can claim this tenfold return. From this perspective you are entitled to claim because you are making an investment in God. You should give with a doubtless grateful attitude. Also expect that the return will come to you; be sure that when you claim it you will receive it. In order to claim, you must state just after tithing *"I have received... (ten times the amount given) in return, with good to all concerned. Thank you. Thank you. Thank you"* However, from the viewpoint of this book, giving should always be done without any expectation.

# Chapter 5

# Gratitude

*One upon whom we bestow kindness but will not express gratitude, is worse than a robber that carries away our belongings.*
*Yoruba proverb*

## 1. General aspects

Gratitude is another way to bring about more prosperity in your life; being grateful is a simple but powerful tool, which is generally overlooked. You should always be appreciative for all the things you have in your life, even the most trivial ones. This quality is highlighted by all religions and indigenous groups.

Besides, gratitude is a very important energy booster that helps manifest your desires much more quickly. When you are grateful for what you have, the universal forces will provide you with even more. In other words, the famous philosopher Plato stated *"a grateful mind is a great mind that eventually attracts to it great things"*. By being thankful you are actually unblocking the flow of all good things, in order that they come to your life. In that sense, gratitude has an immense attracting and transforming power.

It does not matter if you are thankful for big or small things, everything counts. You should be more aware of all the things you can be grateful for. In that sense, thankfulness is naturally related to thoughtfulness. You must regularly practise being grateful with the universe for everything you have, such as:

Your health (albeit you may not have the best health conditions; if you can read this book you are healthier than a lot of people in the world).

The money that you have (although it may not be the amount that you desire).

The job you have (although it may not be the ideal one).

Other things (relatives, friends, the place where you live, the food that you eat, etc.).

You can also be thankful for the unique features of your character, your distinct personal characteristics, your body and mind, the people you deal with, any object you own, and places you have been and your past experiences (such as work activities, spiritual events, artistic shows, meetings with friends, family reunions, etc.). All your statements regarding gratitude should be heart-felt, and not a mere mechanical recitation of words.

Thankfulness is a very effective tool that helps you attract more good things in your life. Each time you are grateful you are raising your energy levels and, in turn, you invite in more positive situations, people and things to your life. Besides, when you are appreciative you cannot feel sad, complain or moan. Gratitude cancels out any negative emotion with its transmuting power. The best way to be thankful is to use gratitude statements. You can focus on what you like in your life and then say: *"I like... because... Thank you, Universe (or God)"*.

When you are grateful there is no opposition to the manifestation of your desires. In fact, by being thankful, you actually generate vibrations in alignment with the objects you want to materialise. You should be thankful even about the things you take for granted, such as that you can breathe, you can have a shower, you are alive, etc.

The frequent use of this technique will help you identify areas in which you are currently prosperous, albeit in some cases to a very little extent. When you ennoble what you have, you pave the way to greater gifts. In that effect, gratefulness is the opposite to being conditional and speculative.

It's important to highlight that you should also express your gratitude to people close to you. You must be appreciative for the advice, support, information or any other gifts that you receive from them. When you have this attitude, they are likely to feel more important; your gratitude will raise their self-worth. As a consequence, they are also likely to spontaneously do even more for you in the future. Try to use praise or compliments whenever possible; those little things make a difference.

It was said that by having a grateful attitude you eliminate resistance regarding the manifestation of your desires. Everyone benefits from gratitude, if you are thankful, you will lift you own mood and others.

## 2. Gratefulness regarding money

It's important to pinpoint that thankfulness is a welcoming attitude towards money. When you are grateful you tend to attract more money in your life. For this reason, you should always be thankful in relation to the money you have, even in the case that it is very little. From the metaphysical perspective, when you are grateful for the money you have, it will naturally multiply.

Bear in mind that you should never be thankful because you feel obligated to do so. On the contrary, your attitude of gratitude should always be unconditional. When you have this gratitude attitude, you are recognising the generosity of the universal forces with you, and they in turn will provide you with more things. In that sense, by being thankful, you tune in with the unlimited all-powerful supply.

It's important to be grateful, even in the moments that you don't receive money or you are short of it. In those cases, you can also ask yourself: *"Which is the gift hidden in this situation?"*, *"How can I improve it?"* or *"What are the things that I can feel appreciative about this"*. At the same time, be confident that your bad economic circumstances are just temporary, not permanent. Be faithful that your financial situation will improve and you will see that it will certainly do so.

Always be grateful for the material things that you have, such as your properties, funds and any other belongings. You must thank the Universe for everything you own, even though you might not have the objects of your desire yet. This type of attitude will help you manifest your dreams much more easily. By being thankful for what you have, your desires (that is to say, what you don't have yet) are likely to materialise more quickly.

In order to have a prosperous mindset, you must get used to being grateful. This type of mentality gets you closer to the unbounded universal forces. In that effect, thankfulness is opposite to scarcity thinking. Gratitude is also contrary to competition mindset, which makes you believe that you can only get more money if others have less.

It was explained that when you thank the Universe you actually broadcast very high vibrations. With gratitude all your thoughts are oriented toward the positive aspects of your reality, dismissing negative ones.

At the same time, by being thankful, you implicitly state that you trust the universe. As a consequence of this, the universal forces will reward you with new gifts. Being grateful always makes you more faithful and, in turn, wealthier.

## 3. Exercises to practise gratitude

### A. Gratitude journal

The gratitude journal is a frequent recording of all things you are grateful for. The use of this technique will bring about more affluence in your life. You can either take these notes in a notepad or use your computer. On a daily basis, you must simply write down a list of all things which you are thankful for. In order to do so, you can use some sentences such as *"I'm grateful for... because... Thank you"* or *"Thank you for having..."* You have to enumerate all the things that come to your mind, even trifling ones. You can also write a whole script that includes everything that you are thankful for. Besides, you can use images to refer to the objects of your appreciation.

## B. Gratitude when you pay bills

Most people tend to feel bad when they have to pay their expenses. Instead, you must get accustomed to feeling appreciative each time you pay others for the goods or services they provide you with. By being grateful you will attract even more goods and services to your life.

You should always be thankful that you can enjoy those goods or services you are paying for. You must also be grateful that other people trust you and provide you with their products and services. The frequent use of this technique will bring about more abundance to your life.

## C. Gratitude before the success of others

There is a very wellknown saying that goes *"What you wish to others, either good or bad, it will come back to you"*. Every time you meet people such as relatives, friends, workmates, partners, acquaintances or even strangers you must be grateful for their achievements. When you have this attitude, you radiate high vibrations, which in turn hasten the materialisation of your dreams.

Most people tend to naturally feel envious before others' accomplishments. It's important to realise that jealousy only generates low vibrations, which pushes away the manifestation of your desires.

For this reason, you should be happy before the attainments of others. Always feel grateful for that, feel good about them. Your positive attitude towards others will make you attract good things to your life.

Besides, you should also be open to receive gratitude from others. Many people tend to be uncomfortable, shy or undeserving when they hear the words "thank you" from others. Instead you should open your heart and receive their gratitude unreservedly. Feel happy about the fact that you are thanked for something that you did, gave or said to them. Moreover feel good that you added some value to other people's lives; you were of contribution to them.

## D. Gratitude and visualisation

When you use the visualisation technique, explained before in this book, you should always thank the universe because your desires are on the way to manifestation. In that sense, by being grateful, you are actually accelerating the materialisation of your dreams.

Besides, when your desires turn up, you should also be grateful. In that case, you are thankful because your dreams have manifested. In relation to visualisation, go to the respective chapter to see the specific techniques.

## E. Blessing

This is a tool which is also connected to gratitude. You must know that blessing brings more affluence to your life. In that sense, you should bless everything that you have in your life. You must bless your body, your family, your money, other belongings, etc. You should also bless any occasional strangers you meet. Bless the future and its forthcoming opportunities. Also bless your past and its experiences and lessons. You should bless rich people and poor people, young people and old ones.

There are several scientific studies conducted by Emoto proving that water molecules exposed to blessings by monks changed their internal structure. Those molecules after the blessings showed a more beautiful structure than before. However, the same water molecules developed ugly internal structures when they were exposed to snide remarks. There is a very important lesson to learn from that experiment. You have to remember that most of your body is made up of water; when you get accustomed to using positive words, its overall structure and functioning will improve.

To put it simply, everything you bless becomes more positive.

Blessing is opposite to criticism and condemnation. Blessing is only positive energy; and on the other side, criticism and complaint represent negative energy. As it was explained before in this book, positive vibrations hasten the manifestation of more prosperity in your life; on the contrary, negative vibrations just push abundance faraway.

If you work or carry out any business activities, a good exercise is to bless everybody you meet in your life. For example, bless your clients and suppliers, debtors and creditors, partners, community, employees, government, etc. Even bless your competitors, wish them the best, rest assured that there is enough for every company in the market. On the other side, if you work for a company as an employee you should bless your workmates and boss; wish them the best.

If you are in the middle of a negotiation process, also bless the interests of both parties involved in it. In that case, try to imagine a win-win solution for the negotiation process, in which both parties have their needs met, and bless it in advance. Try to avoid any scarcity thoughts which supports that you can only win at the expense of the other party.

## F. Admiration

This tool is suggested by many metaphysical masters. You should admire things, people and situations whenever possible. When you admire something or someone, you selectively try to find their beautiful aspects.

You can apply this to things that you naturally admire, such as an awe-inspiring landscape or specific artists that you like. But you can also admire anything such as buildings, cars, people, the sky, children, elderly people, clothes, food, other cultures, etc.

Admiration helps you be in a better mood. Admiring puts you in a state of non-defensiveness. This tool is good to use when you are despondent, disappointed or desolate. Admiring is an easy and practical way to shift your emotions to more positive ones.

When you admire things or people you are radiating good vibrations, which attract more good things to your life. Admiration represents a state of allowance in your life. It is helpful to develop an energetic connection with objects of desire, in order that they can manifest more quickly.

In order to use this tool, you should describe the best traits of things or people in your life. For example, you can use the sentence *"... is good"* or *"I love..."* You can use any other adjectives, such as *"beautiful"*, *"gorgeous"* and any other positive one. You can also justify the good characteristics *("... is good because...")*.

Admiration can even be applied to disgusting things in your life, such as relationships or people, or a negative financial situation. Everything and everyone has a positive side, albeit hidden in some cases. For this reason, you should ask yourself *"What is the good trait of...?"*

Some coaches recommend that you should ask yourself positive questions, both in the morning or before going to sleep. Some examples of these questions are: *"What makes me feel grateful?"*, *"What makes me feel joyous?"*, *"What makes me feel in peace and relaxed?"*, *"What makes me feel loving?"* and *"What makes me feel generous?"* among others. When you use these questions you should focus on the things or people that make you feel those emotional states. But also look at the details of those feelings; for example, ask yourself *"And how do I feel this lovingness?"* All these questions put you in a state of admiration. This state puts you in a high vibration state, which in turn accelerates the materialisation of your dreams.

## G. Celebration

Celebration is another way of being grateful. You must celebrate when you achieve things in your life, even small or trivial ones. You must use this tool even when your accomplishment is different from the one you expected.

All celebration activities are connected to positive emotional states, such as joy, thankfulness, glee, etc. An example is a wedding party where all people are cheerful and elated. When you are elated, you radiate high vibrations, and this, in turn hastens the manifestation of your desires.

There are different ways of celebrating. For example, you can organise events to celebrate things in your life, for example a party or a meeting. However any form of celebration is an overt demonstration of gratitude to the universe. At the same time, celebration is a way of pampering yourself for your good deeds. When you choose to celebrate with other people, you are also sharing your happiness with them.

When you celebrate you must not necessarily engage in expensive activities. Small events, such as a homemade dinner, a barbecue for friends, or eating out with your partner have special meaning too. There are other simple ways of celebrating, such as: buying a gift for you, going on a holiday, having a foot massage, buying new clothes, etc.

Each time you celebrate you are implicitly telling the universe that you are thankful and cheerful about good things you achieved or you have. Besides, you can also celebrate positive things that you didn't purposely attain, but happened to you spontaneously or effortlessly. In any case, celebration makes you attract more good things in your life.

You can keep a record of your accomplishments. Make a list of your recent achievements in a specific journal and update it frequently. This helps you keep track of them, and at the same time, attracts more accomplishments. In that notebook you can also take note of the way you will celebrate each achievement.

# Chapter 6

# De-cluttering

## 1. Tidying up your environment

*It's important to make the connection between your external environment and the way you feel internally, If you live in a mess, you will start to feel like a mess inside.*
*Bernice Walmsley*

### 1.1. De-cluttering and abundance

*Disorderly persons are rarely rich, and orderly persons are rarely poor.*
*Samuel Smiles*

In this materialistic era, people tend to hold on to too many things, most of them unnecessary and bothersome. This common attitude towards material things is supported by companies, which constantly launch new products and implement ingenious marketing strategies to entice customers.

For this reason, you should monitor your abode to see if you keep it in order, neat and equipped only with useful stuff. In fact, the presence of useless things and disorder in your place may be hindering your way to prosperity. De-cluttering is a very simple but also effective tool to attract more prosperity to your life.

You should tidy up the places where you live and work whenever possible. De-cluttering includes keeping your place clean and orderly and getting rid of all things that you don't need. In that sense, Carelyle says that clutter is *"anything that is not loved, not useful or not kept in an orderly manner"*. De-cluttering is an ongoing series of activities and not a one-off task.

De-cluttering is a very relevant action to raise the energy in your environment. Because of this each time you de-clutter your place you eliminate negative energy, which contributes to the manifestation of your desires. You will see that, when you de-clutter on a frequent basis, the amount of money that you get unexpectedly increases.

Cluttering, or hoarding things that are useless or unloved, is a conspicuous sign of attachment, which is linked to a scarcity mentality. By acting this way, you are unnecessarily withholding energy, which hampers the materialisation of your dreams.

It's important to know that, when you clean your place, you are also creating a vacuum, which will attract new things to your life. When you de-clutter you make room for new good things, either material or immaterial, to come to your environment.

It was said before that when you clean and tidy up your place you eliminate resistance to the materialisation of your dreams. At the same time, by de-cluttering on a regular basis you can find actual objects of value in your place and bin those that are worthless.

Some people don't de-clutter because they tend to put off this activity. You may procrastinate because of several reasons, for example you may consider that this task is boring, an effort or time-consuming. You may also be fearful of changing some things in your life; in this case you are strongly attached to the status quo.

In some other cases, de-cluttering may be a confusing activity because you don't know where to start. You may also be disinterested in de-cluttering because it is an activity that does not generate any profits for you. In other cases, you could be in denial; you believe that you don't need to clean up your place; it looks OK as it is. If the last scenario applies, ask for a second opinion about that; close people will provide you with useful insights.

## 1.2. Benefits of de-cluttering

You must get used to keeping your place spotlessly clean and kempt. Tidiness radiates good vibration and supports you in the manifestation process of your desires. It also clears the negative energy stuck in the places. After tidying you are likely to feel the shift in energy, circulating more lightly and lively. In that sense, when you de-clutter your space, you unclog the flow of energy in your environment creating more room to attract new good things to your life.

You should try your best to be a tidy person and de-clutter frequently. An unkempt place is a reflection of negative aspects of your self-image. Make the commitment to put things in order and get rid of useless items. If you spruce up your place you will certainly have a sense of accomplishment, which will boost your self-esteem.

By cleaning up your place you will also save time. You may tend to waste a lot of time trying to find your things in an untidy place. After you de-clutter, by knowing where all your essential things are, you are likely to be more efficient when you have to use them.

In some cases, you may tend to buy things that you forgot you had, because they are lost or mixed up with other stuff. In that sense, by de-cluttering you may save some money. If you are tidy and de-clutter on a frequent basis, you will also have much more room which will make your staying at your place more pleasant.

De-cluttering also prompts you to go beyond your comfort zone and it is a self-empowering activity, albeit sometimes a bit tedious. Sprucing up the environment is also a very effective way to organise your thoughts, and get rid of your mental cluttering. Besides, de-cluttering contributes to improve your self-image, you feel capable of keeping things in order.

By cleaning up your place you are also demonstrating that you can take care of yourself appropriately. That's a very important sign of self-respect and self-love. For all the above reasons, tidying up only brings about positive vibrations, which hasten the materialisation of your dreams

In conclusion, an untidy place obstructs your progress in life. On the contrary, sprucing it up makes room for the manifestation of your desires.

## 1.3. Tips for efficient de-cluttering

Try to devote at least a few minutes to de-cluttering every day if possible. You can also schedule specific hours in your spare time for this purpose. If you are reluctant to take action, you can motivate yourself in different ways. Visualising the details of your place after you have de-cluttered it, making a commitment to an outsider that will control the results of this process and taking baby steps or setting sensible deadlines are some strategies. What is important is to take action. In that effect, Walmsley says that *"clutter increases, and increases, in direct proportion to the amount of time we choose to ignore it"*.

It's important to have all the resources necessary for these tasks in hand. For this reason, get some big carton boxes, plastic bags, scotch tape and cleaning products to use in the de-cluttering tasks. In some cases, you will also need help from your close people, for example, when the place is too untidy or some things are difficult to be moved on your own.

Look for the places where junk is accumulated and take action as soon as possible. You should begin to spruce up the easiest room in your place. You can also give priority to rooms that are obviously dingy, cramped or dark. Pay close attention to objects hampering the traffic throughout your house or workplace.

It's important to rid yourself of any clothes or objects not used for a while. Throw away broken objects that are difficult to repair or outdated stuff. By getting rid of useless things, you are eliminating bad energy from your place, which in turn, dissolves the blocks in the manifestation process of your desires.

When you tidy up, you clear up the energy. All unnecessary or worthless objects you keep consume part of your vital energy. You should be wise and only keep essential objects. When you hoard objects, your energy slows down and it is much more difficult to attract things that you desire.

In some cases, you just keep useless things because of the level of emotional attachment to these objects. A very interesting way to discard things is to assess how your mood is when you are in contact with each object. You have to ask yourself *"Does this make me feel alive?"* or *"Does this make me feel at ease and light?"* If your answer is no, this is a very important sign that the object must be discarded.

A very well-known method to tidy up your stuff is to make three piles. The first one will include all things to be thrown away. The second will enclose things to be analysed in detail later, or interim pile. The third one will have things to be kept; this stuff is loved, functional or useful, in some way. The objects that made up the third pile should be kept in an orderly manner. In order to do so, you can use boxes or files with labels to identify their contents.

Some say that the floor at your place should be kept as free as possible. There should not be any objects scattered on it, in order to avoid financial problems.

You should also look for documents, junk mail, clothes, leaflets, magazines, articles, products, gifts or souvenirs with no meaning in your life. You must get rid of them as soon as possible. All stuff that is classified as clutter can be a) disposed as garbage b) sold as second hand items or c) donated to charities and social organisations.

Walmsley states that if you don't feel secure about keeping some stuff or binning it, you can put in a box with scotch tape with a label saying that it should be opened in three weeks' time. Then you have to check on the specific date, if that box was not opened in the meanwhile, that stuff can be considered useless and disposable. You can set different deadlines for different types of stuff.

From the metaphysical perspective, it's better to donate (option c) stuff that is useless or worthless, because someone with fewer resources is benefited from those things. As it was explained before in this book, when you are giving things away, like in the case of donating, you are also raising your energy, and, in turn, this will accelerate the manifestation of your desires.

You should also clean out your wallet, purse, bag or briefcase. When you do so, throw away worthless or outdated stuff. At your place, keep the receipts, bills and other documents in order, with a sensible filing system. You must also clean up your computer, by eliminating files, folders, programmes or e-mails that are useless or old. It's also important to keep all the information in your PC organised by using an easy-to-use system of folders for it.

You should discard any worthless and superfluous stuff on a regular basis. The same applies to your car, get rid of any useless stuff in it and keep it clean.

Another point to highlight is the stuff that is useful should be kept in a tidy state. In order to do so, once you use things, get accustomed to putting them back in the right place. Your important things, or the ones that you use frequently, can be kept in boxes of files with a clear label describing their contents. These boxes and files should be analysed and cleaned up on a continuous basis.

## 2. Emotional, corporal and mental de-cluttering

*The type of thought that we entertain both creates and draws the conditions that crystallize about it...*
*Ralph Waldo Trine*

Although some of these topics will be explained more in detail over this book we will briefly mention some of their main aspects. In relation to emotional de-cluttering you should be aware of any negative emotion that you resist to let go. Some methods like Sedona, tapping system and others can provide you with very powerful techniques to get rid of negative emotions.

As an example, you can imagine events or facts that upset you and feel the negative emotions related to them. After that, imagine releasing those negative emotions. See them as if they went away from you. You can picture them as clouds or as smoke flying away in the air. By practising forgiveness, generosity and gratitude you will shift your emotions to more positive ones.

Secondly you also have to tidy up your thoughts. Some activities such as meditation, yoga, cutting down on media, being in contact with nature, dancing, camping or listening to pleasant music will help you de-clutter your mind. When you replace your negative beliefs for more positive ones, you are also cleaning up your mind. Instead, each time that you worry, complain or procrastinate, you are reducing your valuable mind energy.

Lastly, cleaning up your body can be addressed in different ways, most of them very well known. There are many activities that you can try such as a diet, fasting, eating organic or natural food, practising exercise or sports, sauna, massage, visiting a chiropractor, among others. All of them are relevant to de-cluttering your body.

# Chapter 7

# Meditation

## 1. General effects of meditation

*Meditation is just to be, not doing anything – no action, no thought, no emotion. You just are and it is sheer delight.*
*Osho*

Meditation is another important tool to attract prosperity. Meditation is an empirical process that lessens your mental and physical tension. When you meditate regularly, you will notice that your body becomes lighter and relaxed. With meditation, you can enjoy a state of passiveness in which you temporarily turn off your ever-working mind. Frequent practice of meditation places you in a non-rational state; you will feel that your entire being goes beyond your mundane circumstances.

Besides, meditation improves your circulation, the working of your organs and nervous system. This practice also lowers your brainwaves and normalises your heart rate. Meditation also replenishes your body from exhaustive activities. All these positive physical effects have been certified by plentiful medical research. In short, meditation is a very complete discipline that helps you obtain serenity and plenitude. In those states you naturally radiate positive vibrations, which accelerate the materialisation of your desires.

It's important to highlight that all meditation techniques lead you to physical relaxation. In that sense, relaxation is the ideal state in which your mind can make use of its most powerful resources. When you practice meditation frequently you will feel as if you are a channel or conduit for the manifestation of universal forces.

When you meditate your mind works more at ease because you reduce the levels of stress. Stress generally affects the functioning of the body and mental processes. Stress is the consequence of facing threatening situations (real or imaginary) and the main cause of many illnesses. Meditation helps restore your natural state of equilibrium; it rebalances your mind energy. In a meditative state, you are likely to feel, for example, more capable of visualising the objects of your desire.

When you meditate you are in a state of relaxation but at the same time alert. Meditation makes you enter a state of timelessness and restfulness. When you practice meditation you regularly feel your interconnectedness with everything,

It's important to highlight other positive effects of meditation.

It frees you from extraneous and disruptive thoughts and disturbing emotions. As a consequence of this, you can gain more clarity about problematic situations. In that sense, calmness, and not languor, is a great source of inner power. When you meditate you can pay attention to the silence; it is a very effective way to be free from your chattering mind.

Meditation also prompts you to have more intuitive insights and creative thoughts, which drive you to take inspired actions. Mediation is a tool that makes you more receptive to intuitive signals, like images or sensations. This is possible because meditating takes you away from a routine form of thinking and, instead, allows you to have a wiser perspective on facts.

The practice of meditation lifts your vibrations; you are achieving high and pure ones. This is beneficial for the clarification of your objectives and the manifestation of your desires. It also empowers the use of visualisations or affirmations. Meditation also makes you more aware that you are connected to the all-mighty universal forces.

It also helps withdraw your awareness from the current negative circumstances (for example, lack of money or scarcity). This is true because when you meditate your main focus is inside and not outside (your current circumstances).

Meditation also quiets your inner critic, which is chattering at all times. Meditating progressively de-clutters your mind and emotions. When you meditate it helps you empty yourself up; you can achieve a state of peacefulness. This state of peace helps you attract more prosperity to your life.

## 2. Meditation procedure

When you meditate you should be patient and detached from the results. Some state that in order to meditate you don't have to do anything, only have a passive attitude. In that sense, meditation entails no active control of body or your thoughts. It's important to have a perspective of an external observer, looking at your thoughts and emotions from outside, this will gradually stabilise them.

When you meditate you should feel as relaxed as possible. Your limbs should be uncrossed. Be aware of any emotional unrest or tension and release it. You can scan your body mentally to see what area of your body is tense and then relax it.

You can affirm or visualise that each part is getting more relaxed. You can also imagine your whole body bathed by a bright light, or a soft substance such as honey. Another way of relaxing your body is tensing your muscles and releasing tension. A third way of eliminating tension is to imagine that it is a passing cloud and that you can let it flee away from your body.

When you meditate your breath and heart rate slow down. You get more relaxed and calm. The minimum time you should devote to meditation is fifteen minutes. This practice should be done every day, preferably after waking up or before going to bed. However it is important that you never meditate as an obligation. Always consider meditation as a fun activity, and not something you must do. When you practise meditation regularly you will feel its accumulated positive effects.

To meditate you should choose a very a quiet room, with no

distractions. Turn off your mobile or disconnect the landline phone in order to remain undisturbed for a while. You can be seated or lie down on the floor or on a bed. If you are lying down, you can keep your knees raised or straight.

The techniques of meditation vary according to different perspectives; however all of them are useful. For example, some masters recommend that, before meditating, you forgive yourself for being uptight and restless. However you can skip this step if you consider it unnecessary.

A common technique of meditation is to relax and concentrate only on your breath. You should focus on your inhalations and exhalations. In that effect, concentrate on the air entering your lungs and going out from them. Try to put your hand on your belly and fill it inflating. You must imagine that the belly is like a jar that, with each inhalation, is filled up, and with each exhalation is emptied.

Always breathe through your nose. The ideal respiration for meditation is diaphragmatic, also called abdominal. Your breathing should be deep (filling and emptying your belly) and slow. For this, check that your abdomen expands and contracts slowly. You can put your hand on your abdomen to see how it inflates and deflates as a balloon.

When you exhale you can also imagine the tightness going out from your body. As it was said before, the meditation process can be accompanied by a mental body inventory. That means that you mentally scan the different parts of the body that are tense, in order to relax them.

The meditation can also be accompanied by the recitation of a mantra. A mantra is a word or sentence repeated rhythmically (not very loud), as if you were chanting. The mantra should be uttered in slow motion and, if possible, in sync with your respiration.

Some well-known mantras are *"ohm"*, *"one"*, or *"peace"*. *"Ohm"* represents the universal sound that connects you to the unlimited source of provision. You can also use *"love"* imagining your body full of loving energy. However, you can also choose any other mantras that make you feel more comfortable. When you use a mantra you can observe any free associations that come up in your mind; if so, observe them in a non-judgmental manner. It's important to know that some people prefer to meditate without using any mantra.

You can also use "visual" mantras. In this case, you imagine an image or symbol with an important meaning for you. You should focus your attention on it and observe if free associations come out. You can also contemplate, with your eyes open, a bright object, such as a candle or lamp. In this case, you must look at the object wordlessly and with no tension. You should be touching the chosen object with your sight.

There are some unstructured ways of meditation that can include pondering on a certain question. In this case, you should repeatedly ponder on an important subject, without forcing any answer to it. You muse about the topic effortlessly and let your mind give you a spontaneous insight regarding it.

You can also implement the visualisation technique when you meditate. You can imagine that a beam of light enters your body from the top of your head, pervades and cleanses your body. You can also see this ray of light coming from the soles of your feet to the centre of the Earth and coming back to you with vital energy. The beam of light can be golden, violet or white. Some recommend the use of a motley beam of light including the colours of the rainbow to enhance your wisdom and health. In all cases, imagine radiating the light out of your body, reaching every person and everything in the world.

Some masters recommend that, when you meditate, you should count your respiration from one to four and then begin again from the start. You inspire and say "one", you expire and say "and", inspire and say "two" and so on.

When you meditate, your attitude regarding your thoughts

and emotions should be an observing attitude. You have to witness your thoughts and feelings, as if you were an outsider, an external observer. Do not judge or label them. However you can imagine them as if they were passing clouds or ascending bubbles. If your mind starts to wander disorderly ask yourself *"What am I focused on?"* and then concentrate again on your breathing.

When you meditate you can also ask the Universe some questions you consider of importance and then be receptive to the answers. Some examples of questions are:

*What is the way to obtain more money?*
*What are the main financial opportunities in hand?*
*What can I take from this current negative situation?*
*How can I be useful in these negative circumstances?*
*How can I perceive the current situation in a more positive manner?*

The answers to those questions could appear during the meditation process or afterwards. The answers can be explicit or direct (specific words) or indirect (through sounds, images, comments, contact with certain books or people, etc.).

From a wider perspective, any trivial activity that you carry out fully concentrating on the present moment could be considered as a form of meditation. By focusing on the activity fully, you enhance your awareness. When you perform an activity with undivided attention, you are unlikely to be dragged away by thoughts relating to the past or the future. You are likely to enter the timeless state of flow, which will be explained later in this book. However, if you are doing that activity, and passing thoughts come up, you can acknowledge them, release them and then re-concentrate on the activity.

## 3. Other techniques of meditation

### A) Japa meditation

This technique is suggested by Fiddes. You should relax your body and focus your attention on a specific point. At the same time, you must press your thumb and forefinger together while you have your eyes closed. You have to visualize the letter A on the left side of the screen of your mind. Then visualize the letter B on the right side. And then see a space in between.

After this, take a deep breath and exhale saying "Ah". When you exhale you must release all the air and only concentrate on that sound. Imagine it is as if that sound reverberated in the room. It also echoes all over your body. Repeat this part twice.

Then continue visualising first the letter B (on the left) and C (on the right) and follow through the complete sequence mentioned before, until you cover 7 to 10 letters. You must feel joy and gratitude during this process. You can also use this state to visualise your goals.

### B) Focus on the breathing

In this type of meditation you just concentrate on your breathing, but in a rhythmical way. There is a way of breathing called rectangular (or 8-4-8-4). First, you inhale slowly while you count up to 8. Secondly, retain the air in your lungs for 4 seconds. Thirdly, exhale slowly counting up to 8. Finally, you retain the breathing without any air for 4 seconds. Then, you must repeat the whole sequence from the start. A variation of this is the respiration known as square breath, which format is 4-4-4-4.

You can also have the alternate breathing. To do so, you must cover your left nostril with your finger and inhale though the right nostril then cover it up and exhale through the left. After this, while you cover your right nostril, inhale through your left one, and then cover it up and exhale through the right, and so on. You must continue with that cycle many times. There should always be one nostril covered and the other uncovered, alternating them in the way explained above. This type of respiration is used in yoga and helps you achieve a state of balance. This helps you radiate high energy and can be used for the visualisation of your desires.

## C) Mind control

This technique was developed by Silva. You must close your eyes and focus them as if they were looking upward at your eyebrow. Then you count down slowly from three to one and you say the word "relax". This way you will enter the alpha mental state. In this state your brainwaves are at a slower level. While you reach this state you must squeeze you thumb and index fingers to anchor that experience so that you can effortlessly evoke it later. You can stay in an alpha state as long as you want. After this you must count up to come back to the normal state. The alpha state is very adequate to get intuitive insights. You can also use that state to programme your subconscious level with more positive beliefs. You can also use this state to visualise and state affirmations.

## D) Self-hypnosis

Self-hypnosis is a tool that you can intently use to be more suggestible to certain ideas. With this technique you get in direct contact with your subconscious mind. In a self-hypnotic state your mind is more receptive to certain thoughts; they can be imprinted on your subconscious more easily. When you are in this state you are aware but, at the same time, you will feel more relaxed, inwardly focused and in peace. The correct way to enter this heightened state will be briefly indicated below.

You can induce yourself into a state of self-hypnosis looking at a candle or bright object. While you do so, you must think or utter some key words such as "relax". You can also say *"When I see this I feel calmer..."* Then you gradually relax all your muscles and breathe deeply *"Now I sleep... now I am going to sleep more deeply".*

You should become more lethargic and relaxed with every breath you take. Then count down from ten to one. To do so, imagine going down on an elevator in a ten-storey building.

Stay in that hypnotic state for while. In this state you can state affirmations, which must be repeated many times to imprint them on your subconscious level. These suggestions must be positive, simple and direct. You can accompany them with images (visualisation). In this case, you should visualise your dreams as if you had achieved them. You should also feel positive emotions supportive to those desires.

You can also imagine that during the hypnotic process you are entering a special place, such as a sanctuary or a natural environment. Then, in order to come back, you must count up to ten. When you do so, state that you will wake up, invigorated and relaxed.

### E) Invoking guides and angels

Some recommend that, during the meditation process, you invoke your angels or spiritual guides to accompany you. You can also invoke the presence of personalities such as extraordinary thinkers, scholars, great men, artists, etc. Some state that you can call the relatives that passed away for advice from them.

In any of these cases, you should only call people that you most admire or love. The main purpose of this is to ask them for guidance. In that sense, you can ask them different questions about how to attract more prosperity. Be receptive to their answers, which may come to you in different ways (such as images, sensations, signs) other than words.

# Chapter 8

# Positive Thinking

## 1. Beliefs about money

*Man is made or unmade by himself: in the armoury of thought he forges the weapons by which he destroys himself; he also fashions the tools with which he builds for himself heavenly mansions of joy and strength and peace. The outer circumstance shapes itself to the inner world of thought.*
*James Allen*

### 1.1. Importance and origin of your beliefs

*Belief, I'm-positive-I-can attitude, generates the power, skill and energy needed to do it. When you believe I-can-do-it, the how-to-do it develops... When the mind disbelieves or doubts, the mind attracts the reasons to support the belief. Doubt, disbelief, the subconscious will to fail, the not really wanting to succeed, is responsible for most failures... Belief is the thermostat that regulates what we accomplish in life... The size of your success is determined by the size of your belief.*
*David Shwartz*

It's important to highlight that, each time you behave with money in certain ways, there is an underlying belief system which supports those actions. For this reason, it's important for you to analyse your specific beliefs about money.

Your beliefs are the internal rules you follow, which are generally accepted in an unquestionable manner. Your beliefs are stored in your mind and tend to be self perpetuating. From the metaphysical perspective, your beliefs are conveyors of energy;

they carry either positive or negative energy, which pervades your thoughts and actions.

Your negative beliefs are in tune with the energy of resistance, which will delay the materialisation of your dreams. On the contrary, your positive beliefs are in sync with the energy of allowance, which will hasten the manifestation of your desires. Some authors such as Esther and Jerry Hicks say that a belief is a vibration practiced for a long time, and the person will only attract things which are consistent with that vibration.

It's relevant to talk about the origin of your belief system. Your beliefs originated in ideas which you accept are true. This does not mean that there must be any correspondence between your beliefs and reality. You allow yourself to hold on to these ideas, and draw conclusions from them. Your beliefs are also energised with intense congruent feelings, which make them look more solid and real. Over time those beliefs become so solidified in your mind, that they are the "truth", your own truth. To put it simply, your tenets are rules or agreements that you set for yourself; they will direct your thinking and feeling over different topics, including money. Some masters will state that your faith is also a state made up of beliefs, in this case, supportive to your dreams.

There are many metaphors that can be used to describe your beliefs. In that sense, your belief-system is like a cage, limiting by nature. Moreover, your beliefs act like a filter; they only allow you to focus on facts and events consistent with them. Your belief system drives your comportment in ways or directions that match it. Your belief system is like the software of a computer, the computer can only be run according to this programme. Robbins states that your beliefs are like the legs of a table, you have certitude about different things based on several experiences you choose to hold onto.

Your beliefs are decrees that are always in force in your life, unless you decide to remove or change them. Your beliefs about prosperity, as any other belief, are usually hidden; however they drive your behaviour regarding money. If your beliefs about money are positive, they are the main motivators that make you thrive. If your beliefs about abundance are negative, they become your main obstacles to achieving prosperity. These guidelines have different origins. In fact, you have learnt about how to deal with money from different sources such as:

*Messages from media (TV, radio, newspaper, etc.)*
*Parental programming (advice from parents, for example, teaching you how they behave in relation to money, etc.)*
*Your own past experiences related to money (incidents like your accomplishments and setbacks in relation to money)*
*Friends and acquaintances (their advice and behaviour)*
*Other sources (customs, books, training, economic situation of your country, etc.)*
*Other institutions (church, clubs, government, etc.)*

Be aware that most of the conditioning from your environment may be harmful regarding prosperity. At the beginning of this book, there was a list of common negative connotations about money that circulate in societies, which are accepted by most people.

## 1.2. Your beliefs and prosperity

Be aware that some of your current beliefs about money can actually be counterproductive. In that sense, your detrimental beliefs about money can be blocking the manifestation of prosperity in your life. For example, if you think that you cannot deal with money properly, this idea is based on your limiting belief system, and you are likely to act accordingly, matching your beliefs.

As in the case of any person, your belief system about money is like a concealed collage, which is made up of different models and messages imprinted on your subconscious mind. These beliefs about money enclose different aspects of your relationship with money, such as:

*How to earn money*
*How to save money*
*How to spend money*
*How to invest money*
*How to pool money together*
*How to recover from blunders regarding money*
*How to treat poor and rich people*
*Worries and feelings related to money*
*How to care about money*

All your habits about money are based on your belief system. It's very difficult for you to have new habits, unless your belief system changes.

Your belief system about money shapes your self-image regarding prosperity, and also your overall personality. If you are not prosperous yet, it is very likely that your beliefs are sabotaging your attempts to get more money.

For this reason, a good exercise is to unveil your hidden belief system about money. These tenets are deeply rooted in your subconscious mind. They may be defeating your dreams of being more prosperous. For this reason, you should cast some light on your belief system. It is also important to highlight that, being more aware of your beliefs may put you in a state of defensiveness. You might have been attached to those internal rules for a long time. As a consequence, when you examine your beliefs in detail, you may feel challenged or confused.

When you examine your belief system you may find out that some of your beliefs are totally fallacious. This realisation can be very shocking, mostly when you have never reviewed and confronted your beliefs before. However, you must realise that the conscious analysis of your beliefs is a positive process; it helps recalibrate the wrong ones.

### 1.3. Negative beliefs about money

If you are not aware of your main beliefs, they will keep on driving your life on autopilot. In that effect, any negative beliefs about money will come into play, keeping you from being affluent. If you don't alter your beliefs, they will keep on controlling your life. You can deduce the main aspects of your belief-system regarding money if you use statements such as:

*I cannot afford this...*
*I am not sure if I will earn that amount of money...*
*I will never be rich...*

All the statements above have an underlying belief system that is limiting regarding money. Sentences such as *"I can't...", "I am not sure..."* and *"I will never..."* are clear reflections of a constraining belief system about money. The underlying beliefs related to those statements will be preventing you from becoming prosperous in the future, unless you make the conscious decision to change those negative beliefs.

For this reason, always look for implicit or explicit meanings that you assign to the events or things. This is an indirect way to discover your main hidden beliefs about money. Your beliefs also shape your perception on things; they are the particular map you use to read reality. In that sense, your problems (financial difficulties, etc.) are always perceived (and solved) in accordance to your particular interpretation of them. In fact, you never see things "as they are", but through the lens of your particular beliefs.

Beware if you catch yourself saying things like:

*Life is hard*

*Getting prosperous is difficult*
*Rich people are immoral*

From the previous examples, you can deduce your hidden belief system regarding money. You can guess that the underlying beliefs are all detrimental regarding prosperity.

A good approach to change your negative beliefs about money is to assign new meanings to things and facts, even past experiences. A question that you can ask yourself is *"What other meanings can this have?"* Look for more positive interpretations of facts. All beliefs tend to be generalisations such as in the case of *"Rich people are immoral"*. For this reason, you can ask yourself if there are any exceptions to that sentence.

Your belief-system also affects your expectations about money. When you expect something, you are actually projecting or imagining future scenarios. Your expectations become fortune-telling tools; they have self-fulfilling effects in your life. In accordance with this, Taylor states *"In the battle between desire and expectation, the Universe is far more likely to give what you expect... Your desires are where your wishes are; your expectations are where your beliefs are. And in the formula of destiny creation nothing is much more powerful than your beliefs"* If you expect to receive or earn more money, you will. If you have no expectancy to get more prosperous, chances are you will not.

There are also clues about your beliefs about money in your actions. Your actions are solid reflections of your hidden belief system. You have to analyse how your beliefs are connected to specific actions. For example, if one of your beliefs is *"I will never be rich"* all your actions will tend to avoid any possible action that can make you rich. Because all beliefs are held on subconscious levels, your actions will be driven in that direction almost unwittingly. For this reason, raising your awareness of your negative beliefs is the most important step you can take to correct them.

In that sense, your beliefs forge your particular character and make you act in a specific manner. You should be aware what character you play in the money game. Some possible characters you may be using regarding money are: spender, saver, investor, victim, waster, stingy, hopeless, carefree, neophyte, knowledgeable, among others.

According to this you will find that some "scenes" in your life are repeated continually; your character is playing them over and over. You will see that your own character tends to interact with specific types of characters. Besides, your character is likely to be more enticed by certain sorts of plots and theatrical genres (such as *"comedy"* or *"financial happiness"*, *"tragedy"* or *"financial turmoil"*, etc.). Your own character will also express specific feelings (such, as glee, desperation, fear, etc.) and use a certain language (*"Money is unlimited"*, *"There is not enough money"*, etc.) when it refers to money onstage.

Ask yourself *"What are the reasons to keep this character?"*, *"How can my actual character perform better regarding money?"* and *"What other roles can I play on the money stage?"*

## 1.4. Exercises to better your belief system

Find below some exercises that can improve your belief system regarding money.

You must know that you can always unlearn and replace any obsolete belief about prosperity. In order to do so, you must be open to new perspectives related to abundance. For example, you can make an overarching list of your main beliefs about money. By writing this list you will discover the main belief about money, which you have chosen in the past unwittingly or consciously. Read the list and ask yourself *"Do these beliefs hinder or allow me to attract more money?"* Then replace all restrictive beliefs about money for more empowering ones, which represent your true essence. After this, forgive yourself for having had those erroneous beliefs. Be open-minded and experimental because all your beliefs, even the most ingrained, are changeable.

Realize that holding on to your disempowering old beliefs is always your choice. Ask yourself some challenging questions such as: *"What are the positive and negative aspects of not having money?"* This question will provide you with a very useful insight about your belief system.

You can also use affirmations about money. This tool will be explained later in this book. An example of an affirmation is *"I am on my way to becoming more prosperous"* Repeat the affirmations frequently to replace the outdated belief.

Look for other perspectives when you think about money. Look for other meanings about it. For example, you can ask yourself: *"How would a rich person think about this?"* This type of question will help you be more creative and challenge your longstanding assumptions.

Don't take your beliefs for granted, even if you have been holding on to them for a while. Challenge them whenever possible, they may be totally obsolete or not applicable any longer.

Try to question the beliefs imposed by your environment such as media, family and friends, etc. Realise that you are generally influenced by social programming. Some questions such as *"Is that belief consistent with me?"* or *"Is that belief actually true"* will help you defy the conditioning coming from your environment.

Ask yourself about your deservedness regarding money. Some questions such as *"Do I feel worthy in relation to money"* and *"Am I willing to receive more money"* will bring you an interesting insight into your self-image regarding money. If you feel unworthy or unwilling, ask yourself about the reasons for that.

You can also reframe your bad experiences with money from a different perspective. Some ways to do so is by asking *"In what other ways I can interpret this?", "What is the positive aspect of this event?"* or *"What was the main contribution of that experience to my evolution?"* This type of question will help you reshape your belief system.

Some sages suggest that you can also change your disempowering beliefs by asking for help from angels or guides. These spiritual beings are always willing to support you to transmute your negative beliefs.

Another important tool is to make a list of expectations about money. In order to do so, you can ask yourself, for example *"How much money am I willing to receive during...?"* When you answer that question, try to go beyond your comfort zone. You can ask that question on a frequent basis to expand your expectations gradually, and in turn reformulate your belief system. Also ask if some of your expectations about money are truly yours. Some of your expectations may be, in fact, related to your close group (family, friends, couple, etc.) or other people (colleagues, organisations, etc.).

Write down your past story about money. Try not to miss any details, include blunders and failures regarding money. Ruiz states *"Ninety-five percent of the beliefs we stored in our minds are nothing but lies, and we suffer because we believe all these lies"* So always doubt those stories. Try to rewrite your story, in a way you wish it would have been. Write your ideal story about money, supposing that in the past you had had all the resources you needed, such as information, technical skills, funds, affection, support, etc. Then imagine that you project this perfect past story on your present and future.

There is a very well known principle called 80/20, which means that 80 per cent of your problems about money (or most of your financial difficulties) come from 20 per cent of your beliefs (or very few of them) So according to this perspective, there are only a few negative beliefs preventing you from having money. You must find out what these core beliefs are, in order to replace them as soon as possible. Once you discover your main negative beliefs, you can also ask yourself *"What are the main payoffs of holding these core disempowering beliefs?"* This question will help you let go of those detrimental beliefs. Don't pay attention to the rest of your beliefs, because they are unimportant.

Your doubts about how to deal with money are also supported by negative beliefs. In this case, your negative beliefs are accompanied by a cause. For example, you may say to yourself *"I am not sure if I can do this because..."* and *"I cannot do this because..."* Explore the reasons why you cannot fulfil your objectives. Then you must challenge those beliefs and replace them with positive ones. You can also look for examples of people that achieve similar goals; you can consider these people as models to emulate.

Have a closer look at your beliefs about money. Analyse if there is a belief that is discordant with the rest of them. It is important that all your beliefs about money are aligned. Your beliefs should be working as if they were members of an effective team; each belief should be cooperating with the rest.

An indirect way to discover your beliefs is to examine in detail the things that you reject. These things are the ones against your belief system. This is an indirect way to examine your belief system. Analyse the things you tend to deflect more thoroughly; you might discover that they were not as detrimental as you thought.

Another way to notice your own beliefs about money is to have a close look at your criticisms to things or people. When you criticise others, you are likely to be projecting your unwanted or unrealised traits on other people. Ask yourself *"How do my criticisms to others apply to me?"*

Your beliefs about money are contracts or agreements you made in the past. Write down a new contract with yourself with empowering conditions regarding money issues. For example, you can state in this new agreement that you want to be financially independent and very prosperous. Your words in that agreement will be your new bond to which you commit undeservedly. Sign this contract and keep it in a safe place.

Examine this agreement frequently to remind you of the new conditions. Be unwaveringly committed and respectful of the terms and conditions of this covenant.

You can ask other questions about money. For example, you can ask yourself *"Where do my beliefs about money come from?"*, *"What are the main conflicts about money because of this belief?"* or *"How do my beliefs about my money affect my emotions and performance?"* This type of question will provide you with very interesting insights into your belief system.

Remele suggests a very interesting NLP technique to deal with beliefs. According to this perspective we have a place in our minds for our beliefs and a place in our minds for doubts. What is a belief is not a doubt and vice versa. In order to apply this technique you should try saying your name and see the place you assign in your mind for that belief. When you say something that, in your opinion, is true, you also use certain posture, movements and facial expressions. So if you say *"I'm a millionaire"* when you are not, you would find a specific place in your mind for that doubt. After this, try to say that affirmation again (*"I'm a millionaire")* but in a relaxed and comfortable posture. You should be breathing deeply and feeling your inner power. While you do so, try to locate this affirmation (*"I'm a millionaire")* in the place of belief (the same place you discover when you said your own name). Accompany this with the same movements, posture and facial expressions that you would use if that affirmation was actually a belief. Repeat it many times. This will change your belief system, installing new beliefs into it.

## 2. Positive thinking

*To look upon the appearances of poverty will produce corresponding forms in your mind, unless you hold the truth that there is no poverty; there is only abundance.*
*Wallace Wattles*

## 2.1. Thoughts always produce effects

*Your positive, optimistic thoughts add to your good more dramatically than compound interest increases your bank savings.*
*Eric Butterworth*

According to the law of cause and effect, every fact or event in your life has specific causes originating them. In some cases, those causes are completely unknown. When you have financial problems, you should discover the negative thoughts that are the main cause of those difficulties. Once noticed these thoughts should be replaced by positive ones.

From a metaphysical perspective, you always attract what you think about more frequently. For this reason, it's very important that, from now on, you only hold stainless thoughts in your mind. If you keep on thinking about your negative economic situation and constantly moan about it, you will end up attracting more alike circumstances. On the contrary, if you have positive thoughts about money you will attract more beneficial situations.

It's necessary to realise that recollections, complaints, dreams, admiration, guesses or musing are all ways of thinking. Your thoughts, either good or bad, are always shaping your reality. From this viewpoint, you can only change your economic circumstances from inside-out.

So if you turn your negative thoughts into more positive ones your circumstances will follow through accordingly. For this reason, your mind acts like a double-edged sword; it can attract good things or bad ones. What you currently see in your life is dependent on the quality of the thoughts that you hold.

For this reason, it is crucial not to focus on any negative event such as poverty, unemployment, crime, and so on. In that effect, you must avoid the news in the media, which can make your thinking negative, without you even noticing.

Besides, you should never focus on lack, for example, the money that you do not have. Instead, always concentrate on the things that you do have. You must also focus on your dreams, bearing in mind the desired end results for them. For example, you can entertain thoughts like *"I am having an X amount of pounds by..."* When you think about your dreams about money, trust that they will certainly be materialised. Always be confident in the Universe, which will provide them in a perfect fashion.

Do not focus on your past failures or shortcomings regarding money. Negative thoughts attract detrimental conditions into your life and make you overlook opportunities. Recall only the positive experiences about money you had in the past. Concentrate on your strengths and not on your weaknesses regarding money. Make a list of all positive things in your current reality; this will help shift your thoughts to more positive ones.

## 2.2. Some tips for positive thinking

### a) Monitor your inner voice

You might have discovered that there is an inner voice harassing you with negative messages about money at all times. This voice is your inner critique. In some cases, this inner narrator has contradictory voices. If what you hear inside your head is not supportive to your prosperity, you must replace that voice for something more constructive. In order to do so, treat the negative murmuring as if it was noise in your head and imagine that it gradually fades away. You can also ridicule your inner voice, changing its tone to a funny one. You can also give peripheral attention to your inner critique; treating it as if it was a bratty child.

### b) Cancelling bad thoughts

Every time that a negative thought appears in your mind, you must immediately cancel it out. In order to do so, you can firmly say to yourself "away", "delete" or "stop". You can use any other word that proves effective to you. You can also replace the negative thought by the same opposite one. For example if your thought is *"I will never be rich"*, you can replace by *"I can be rich"*. Mohr states that your negative patterns and situations in your life can also be dissolved by stating *"I make a stronger commitment to my-self"*

Another point to highlight is that there is no such thing as scarcity; this concept is just mental fabrication, which in turn will be reflected in your circumstances. When you feel that something is lacking in your life, have a close look at your thoughts and emotions, they are likely to be out of alignment with the object of your desire. If so, change them to more positive ones.

### c) Look for pleasurable activities

There are some activities that will naturally prompt you to have more positive thoughts. Some of them may be, for example, playing board games or sports, being in contact with nature, relaxation and meditation, jogging, among others. These activities will vary from one person to another. Look for activities that provide you with some fun time. Because your thoughts and emotions are interconnected, when you experience good feelings you tend to have a more positive mindset. In that sense, when you do these amusing activities you will radiate more positive vibrations that will help you manifest your desires.

### d) Act "as if"

In order to have more positive thoughts about money you can use the technique called "as if". According to this perspective, in order to be a prosperous person, you should be acting as if you were prosperous. By acting "as if" you will bring about better thoughts and this, in turn, will attract more positive circumstances to your life. The use of this technique may help you reformulate your limiting beliefs, replacing them with more allowing ones.

For example, you can act as is you were rich, by feeling more self-assured and confident about money. You can also look for new opportunities for investment. You can be grateful for the money you have and expect to have more.

This tool is very effective because your subconscious mind cannot detect if something is imaginary or real. So your subconscious, where all your beliefs are stored, will end up accepting your way of doing things. As a consequence of this, your belief system will be affected positively.

## e) Saying yes

There is another simple technique you can apply when you realise that you are negative with money. Each time you receive or give money, repeat the word "yes" many times in your mind. The term "yes" is very empowering, with very high vibration. The frequent use of this word will gradually dissolve any resistance to prosperity.

## f) Self awareness

It is important to be very aware of what you think. Your thoughts are energy, either good or bad; they actually transform your reality. Always be vigilant of the thoughts that inhabit your mind. You must also be aware of the words you frequently use; in that sense, your words are the results of your thoughts.

Pay close attention to your vocabulary. It is the actual expression of your thoughts and it should be meticulously chosen. Always monitor your mouth; negative words impact on subconscious and mould your reality. You should always try to have a positive talk. A good way to test your talk is by asking yourself *"Is there any condemnation or complaint in my talk?"* The main aspects of your vocabulary will be elaborated in detail later.

## g) Take note of positive things

Take note of the positive aspects of your day. Talk only about positive things that happened to you or to other people. This is the opposite of gossiping or criticising. When your speech is positive, you will feel more excited and, in turn, you will attract more good things into your life.

Another way to have positive thoughts is to recall good experiences in your life. For example, remember the times you were good with money or you earned money. Try to recall these experiences on a frequent basis. You must be selective with your recollections, allowing only the positive ones to come back to your mind. In this way, you generate higher vibrations, which will hasten the materialisation of your dreams.

## h) Be open to new perspectives

It's important to have a more positive perspective on things, mostly if your current view on the circumstance is gloomy. For example, consider any financial crisis in your life as an opportunity to prosper. A question that you can ask yourself is *"What other meanings does this have for me?"* This question will provide you with great insights.

A very important thought that allows you to have a more positive attitude is that *"Difficulties are always temporary and I can trust my resources completely to deal with any situation"*. In that sense, think that humankind has given enough proofs over time that nothing is insurmountable. You can also bear in mind the saying that goes *"Many good things can happen in my life"*.

## i) Take the driver seat

You are in control of your life; you are more powerful than you think. You are not a vulnerable child dragged down by circumstances. In order to take more control in your life, regularly use sentences like *"I choose..."*, *"I decide..."*, *"I intend"*, *"I adore"* among others. All these statement come from a proactive perspective.

The frequent use of this type of statement will make you radiate positive vibrations, which will hasten the manifestation of more money in your life.

## j) Have a look at your blocks

When you want to overcome your money blocks, you should never use negative statements such as *"I don't want to be poor"*. Instead, you should use positive wording such as *"I want to be rich"*. Your subconscious mind does not recognise the word *"no"*. So when you say *"I don't want to be poor"*, your subconscious hears *"I want to be poor"*.

Besides, by identifying what you do not want (for example *"I don't want to be poor")* you can define what you want (*"I want to be rich"*). Each time that you find something that you don't want ask yourself *"What do I really want?"* Bear in mind that what you don't want is likely to be the opposite of what you want.

## k) Daydreaming

Hicks states that a good sentence to generate positive thoughts is *"It would be very good that..."* This type of sentence prompts you to daydream about your innermost desires. In that effect, you should always think big; depict your ideal scenarios and their unlimited possibilities. In this way, you can experience more positive emotions and radiate high vibrations, which in turn attracts the desired situations or objects to your life.

## l) Focus on the present moment

If you are like most people, you are likely to be worried about money issues. In that effect, Tolle states that worries are a dysfunctional consequence of being too focused on the future and resisting the present moment. This author gives some interesting tips for this state of negativity. If you have negative thoughts about money, you should observe them as if you were a neutral outsider or an impartial watcher.

You can also listen to your internal critique as an external beholder in an impartial way. Besides, you should be aware of your emotions and physical sensations, with no judgement, as if you were an impartial watcher.

According to this perspective, your emotions and thoughts are passing by nature, and if you treat them this way, they will go past naturally. Another suggested way to achieve a state of stillness is focusing completely on the task at hand, not considering it as a means to an end.

### m) Monitor your energy

You always pick up thoughts and emotions, which are made up of energy, from different places you have been. If you notice that your thoughts or feelings are negative, you should ask yourself *"Is this energy mine?"* If the answer is "*no*", let the negative energy go away. In order to do so, imagine the negative energy going out of your body and mind, as a passing cloud. Later in this book you will see more detailed techniques to manage your energy more effectively.

### n) State that good things are to come

According to this perspective Michael Losier suggests that, once you have discovered what you truly want (your desires), you should write down some positive statements related to the things that you want to manifest. The use of this tool will make your thoughts more positive.

An example of this statement could be *"I am on the way to attract* (you must enumerate the things that you want)... *and what I like about this object of desire is...* (you must also state the positive reasons and feelings that make you want to have that). You can finish the statement like this *"The Law of Attraction is orchestrating what is necessary for this to materialise"*. With this type of statement you are allowing your dreams to manifest, you are in alignment with the almighty universal forces. By stating this, you also think that it is possible. When you say or write these sentences, you must remain relaxed and calm.

## o) Recognize the connection between thoughts and feelings

You must bear in mind that your thoughts are always connected to your feelings. For this reason, be aware of your feelings. Never suppress them; instead let them go whenever possible. All negative emotional states such as fear, hesitation or doubt drain your vital energy.

When you experience negative feelings, those states hinder the materialisation of your dreams. This happens because those emotions radiate negative vibrations that push prosperity away. Instead, when you have positive emotions events orchestrate in accordance to your dreams. Later in this book, you will see some techniques for efficient emotional management.

## p) Question your thinking regularly

On a frequent basis, you should ask yourself helpful questions to challenge your thinking. These types of questions will help you discover hidden aspects of your thoughts in relation to money. Some examples of questions are:

*What does money represent to me?*
*What's a prosperous person for me?*
*Am I on the right path regarding money?*
*Do I have any limit in my income?*
*Why do I have little money?*
*How am I emulating my parents regarding money?*
*What type of person should I be if I was prosperous?*
*What beliefs should I need to have more money?*
*Do I actually love money or repel it?*

## 3. Procrastination

### 3.1. Reasons for procrastination

Procrastinating is a particular way of thinking, albeit a negative one. When you procrastinate you decide not to do some thing at present, with the "promise" to do it, instead, in the future. Procrastinating radiates negative energy which hinders the manifestation of your dreams. In fact you may be postponing important things such as some actions leading to the attainment of your innermost desires. In that effect, you may be procrastinating for different reasons:

*Lack of motivation*. You may feel tired, apathetic, lazy, bored or despondent when you have to take action.

*Excessive planning*. You plan too much. This implicitly means that you are looking for perfection.

*Focus on short-term gratification over long-term*. You prefer pleasurable activities at present rather than taking the step towards results that will show up in the future.

*Daydreaming*. You are constantly thinking how things would be, without taking any initiative to go for your dreams.

*Fortune-telling mindset*. You don't take action at present, because you imagine the worst outcome possible for your performance.

*Fear*. You can be fearful either of success or failure. In the case of fear of failure, you don't take action to avoid the frustration you will experience if everything goes wrong. In the case of fear of success, you don't take action because you imagine yourself overwhelmed in the case that things go well; in your inner heart you don't feel capable of managing the consequences of your success.

## 3.2. Main implications of procrastination

When you procrastinate you do not take action because you are resisting something. You may be postponing activities that can make you more prosperous. For this reason, you should look for signs of emotional resistance regarding money. In that effect, procrastination always entails immobility or resistance to change. Postponing things is a blatant sign of mediocrity in your life. It is one of the most relevant factors against the prospering flow.

You may think that it is better to act in the future in a positive way, instead of taking action now. However ask yourself the question below to know if you are actually postponing some activities that can make you generate more money.

*What negative beliefs about money should I be getting rid of?*
*What actions am I afraid to take to be more prosperous? What happens if I take those actions?*
*Why am I avoiding looking for opportunities to make money?*
*What are the main benefits of not taking any action at present?*
*What are the advantages of not being prosperous?*
*What are the ideas that need to be explored in detail at present regarding money?*
*What habit should I change that will benefit my financial situation?*
*What resources should I obtain to improve my financial skills?*
*What people should I contact to have support for my financial projects?*
*What messages from my intuitive part am I not following?*
*What type of metaphysical activities (visualisation, meditation, etc.) should I carry out to raise my vibrations and attract more money?*

It's important to highlight that if you are too cautious when you have to take any action, you are likely to lose a lot of opportunities. The key factor to overcome procrastination is being proactive, just do it, don't second guess. You should take the initiative, begin with baby steps and then continue firmly and steadily.

### 3.3. Effective ways to eliminate procrastination

Some easy ways to avoid procrastination in relation to prosperity are:

*Schedule your activities related to money:* This can include making a sensible to-do list in relation to the generation of more money in your life. Those activities don't necessarily have to be big ones; even small actions will do well. For example, you can schedule some time to meditate and visualise your goals. Don't think about doing things "someday". Have a committal attitude and set realistic deadlines for each outstanding task. Don't pressurise yourself; remember that things in the Universe work effortlessly. You can classify those activities in different categories, such as priority, less important and irrelevant. Focus primarily on the priority ones.

*Observe your progress in your activities:* Keep records of all your achievements regarding money and celebrate them in a pleasurable manner. Also be grateful with the Universe for those accomplishments. Relish in good feelings because of having been proactive.

*Try to visualise the outcomes of taking actions:* Use the visualisation techniques explained in this book. You should be visualising not only the end results that you want to obtain, but also see yourself taking inspired action. On the other hand, have a quick peripheral look at the negative consequences of not taking actions, but don't dwell on this too much, because you don't want to attract that. This will boost your mood to go ahead with your tasks.

*Don't look for perfectionism:* All things are perfectible, even the way of becoming a prosperous person. For this reason, if you feel you have to take any action, don't try to delay it until you guess the ideal way to perform it. Just do things the best way possible and the universal forces will support you unconditionally. The Universe will gradually show you the rest of the way ahead. You should put down the voice of your inner critique when you feel that you are looking for perfection.

*Have a break:* After you carry out things that you used to procrastinate over, give yourself a break-time to recharge your batteries. Don't only focus on action, have fun. Pace yourself out, never overwork; remember that the universe only works with ease.

*Have fun*: Look for the most pleasurable ways to carry out an activity that you tend to procrastinate over. For example, if you don't like to meditate, you can be encouraged to take up this practise by listening to some calming music and lighting some incense. Try to mix up unpleasant activities with pleasurable ones.

*Start with easy tasks:* If you are undecided about activities to begin with, start with the easiest ones. In this way you feel more motivated to continue with the more complex ones.

*Reward yourself*: Plan in advance some rewards to be enjoyed after finishing the procrastinated tasks. In order to keep you motivated tie the unpleasant things to pleasant ones. For example, you can have a relaxing bath, after analysing and setting your financial goals.

*Take the first step:* Just taking action will bring serenity to your mind. Also remember that the almighty universal flow is always backing you.

*Organise your environment:* This means having all the resources that you need for the task at hand, whenever possible. For example, you may be postponing the practise of meditation because you don't have a quiet and tidy room at home. In order to solve this, try to get a room at your house clean and tidy so that it can be used for meditation.

*Take action:* In order not to procrastinate, the best way is just to do things. Don't quit before even considering the possibility of trying. To act effectively you should not get stuck in your thoughts.

*Be committed to your actions:* Make a promise that you will act despite potential difficulties. As it was previously explained, you can draw up a contract, in which you commit to be prosperous. You can also state the actions that you will take in that agreement. This is a very effective way to say "no" to conformity or slothfulness. It's also important to go beyond your comfort zone; this will stretch your mind. For example you can always set higher goals regarding money than in the past.

*Overcome fear:* There will always be fear or doubt in relation to an unfamiliar task; so just take action anyway. For example, if you have not practised meditation before you may be hesitant about its positive effects. Try it many times; it takes time to take up the habit, even a positive one. If you are afraid of doing something, embrace the fear and act all the same. You will realise that actions gradually beat your dread. There is much more power when you take action than when you hold yourself in a state of helplessness.

# 4. Worries

*Poverty is a mental disease.*
*Joseph Murphy*

## 4.1. Main aspects of worries

Worries are dysfunctional thoughts about a future situation that may happen. They can include temporary thoughts up to obsessive ruminations. In any case, you have to grasp that worries are just products of your imagination and not real facts. However, worries represent a very important waste of energy.

Worrying is an unhealthy and immobilising habit that only drains your vital energy. It does not matter how much you worry, in practice, worrying itself does not solve any problem at all.

Worries are parasites in your mind that countermand your positive thoughts. They also cancel out your positive vibrations. In fact, by worrying you are lowering your vibrations, which hinder the manifestation of your desires. To put it simply, preoccupation always repels abundance.

Kennerly states that worries can manifest in different ways, such as: anticipating disasters, black-and-white thinking, searching for the things we fear, generalising, and ignoring the positive aspects of a situation. Some examples of these manifestations applied to money are:

*"What if I lose all my money?"* In this case you are anticipating disasters.

*"There are some people born to be rich and others born to be poor".* This is a black and white reasoning.

*"I have never been good with money"*. Here you are generalising, to counteract this way of thinking you can ask yourself *"Never ever?"*

*"I will look for new jobs in the newspaper just in case I get fired"*. In this case you are looking for the negative (getting fired), instead of focusing on the positive (that you actually have a job).

*"I'm incapable of getting money"* In this case you are dismissing past positive evidences, which are the times that you actually got money. Unless you are a neonate, you surely have some experiences in the past in which you generated more money, at least temporarily.

Beneath all worries there are feelings of fear and doubt. When you worry your capacity to discern any situation, even a simple one, is dramatically diminished. In some cases, when you worry, you tend to act as if you were able to predict the future precisely.

When you worry you tend to use visualisation in a negative way. In that effect, you tend to imagine the worst scenarios for a situation, in some cases with an exhaustive set of details.

You must realise that each time you worry you are focusing on the future. This only represents immobility, lack of power and inaction. The only moment of power to take action is the present one. In fact you cannot take action in the future, only now. For this reason, your worries freeze you up; they set you motionless. They make you powerless, withdrawing you from the only moment of power that is now.

In some cases, worries make you act against your most important objectives. An example, will illustrate this, supposing that you want to set up a business. In this business project you will be carrying out activities that you are good at. In your business, you will be performing tasks that you consider your passion or mission. You also guess that this type of activity will provide you with financial independence, but also with a sense of accomplishment.

Despite that, you don't take action, and continue working for a company as an employee. In that post you feel frustrated because you are carrying out tasks that do not fulfil you as a person. However, you decided not to take any initiative regarding your dreams, which is setting up your own company. You act this way because of your worries, for example you may be scared that your business project will not succeed. You may also be worried about losing all the money invested in that project. All these worries end up immobilising you, and pushing you away from your dreams. Because of your worries, which are imaginary thoughts, you continue working at the company. You have economic security but, because of your worries, you sacrifice the materialisation of your dreams.

## 4.2. Efficient ways to eliminate worries

It was said that the only way you can garner some power over your life circumstances is to focus on the present moment. When you worry your mind is divided; you are so overwhelmed about the potential future circumstances that you cannot act at present. Remember that the present moment is the only point in time of power.

So in order to eliminate worries, you should stay centred in the present moment, as much as possible. Feel your energy field in your body, feel your breathing at this moment. Also be aware that worrying is always a choice of yours. You can be focused on the future or on the present, this is your choice. Find below some other actions to eliminate worries from your life.

A good way to counteract worrying is planning just in case that negative outcome arises. If you use this pre-emptive approach, you are likely to deal with the negative situation more effectively. However many masters will say that if you are expecting negative situations to happen in the future, you are actually attracting them with your expectancy.

Worrying is always linked to uncertain events. You should assess the chance of negative events occurring. Ask yourself *"What is the worst thing that could happen?"* This will put worries in a more realistic perspective.

You can write your worries down on a piece of paper and then destroy it. This is a symbolic way to eliminate your worries and raise your energy.

Relaxing activities and meditation will take worries off your mind. The important thing when you are worried is to raise your energy as much as possible. So by performing calming activities you will radiate more positive vibrations.

If you are worrying that you have many activities, you establish priorities, to deal with them in order of importance. You can start with the easiest task, to feel motivated to go through the rest of them.

Ask yourself *"Is there any hidden reward I will receive if I worry?"* You will find out that worrying is a detrimental way of thinking that only depletes your energy and lowers your vibrations.

Focusing on non-worrying activities can distract your mind from worrying. For example, you can watch movies, play cards, practise sports, or any other fun activity.

If you are apprehensive about not having enough money, trust that the Universe will provide you with it. Don't worry about how things will manifest in your life. Instead surrender to the means and timing of universal forces. Be open to the possibility of receiving money in the most unexpected ways.

Worrying is visualising negative scenarios in the future. So you can use the visualisation techniques to envision positive events and outcomes that replace the negative images related to your worries.

Staying in silence a little time each day. The benefits of staying in silence are highlighted in one of the appendices of this book.

Each time you worry you are focusing on negativity. This brings about negative emotions. You can use a very powerful Neuro Linguistic Programming technique called anchoring. In order to do so, evoke moments in which you experienced good feelings. Then make those images bigger and clearer. Make the sounds and sensations of those past experiences more vivid. Then press your thumb and index finger together to anchor those memories to that physical trigger. Repeat the procedure many times, until you feel that with the pressing of both fingers, you can relive those good emotions.

## 5. Positive posture, gestures and vocabulary
### 5.1. Confident pose

*Acting as if you are wealthy is a powerful tool for attracting what you desire.*
*Lynn Robinson*

There are many scientific studies which certify the direct correlation between physiology and thoughts; in that effect, they condition each other. As a consequence, a good posture affects your thoughts and emotions. A straight relaxed posture puts you in a good mood. Body and mind are intimately integrated, so if you change your posture, you will change your feelings and thoughts.

For this reason, it's important to have a straight posture, not a slouched one. Your gestures should be energetic and brisk. Your walk should not be a sluggish walk, but vigorous. Imagine you walk like a king or a very important person. When you are walking, visualise that your energy covers your way ahead. You can visualise that you are wearing a big long cloak of radiant energy that covers the space you walk in.

If you can get the habits above mentioned you will notice that your thoughts and emotions will become more positive. Because you actually are a mind-body system, your confident posture will prompt you to have positive emotions and thoughts. In turn, your positive feelings and thoughts will radiate good vibrations, which will make the manifestation of your desires easier.

Some recommendations to improve the posture are:

*Try to have a good posture.* Some methods, such as the Alexander system, state that the head is the part of the body that helps you have an ideal posture. In order to do have a good posture, you must relax your shoulders, hips, ankles and knees and lean the head down, leaving your neck relaxed. Then you should lift the head feeling it drag the rest of the energy of the body when it is erect. You must feel the postural energy (originated in the head) going throughout your entire body. From this perspective the head acts like the rudder that controls the rest of the body. When you have a good posture, your thoughts and emotions are to be affected positively, which will raise your vibrations.

*Rehearse your prosperous posture.* Imagine how you would feel physically if you get more abundance in your life. Try to visualise your posture, movements and gestures vividly. You should also use your body to rehearse that state of abundance. If you practise this on a frequent basis you will end up attracting more prosperity into your life.

*Try to always dress smart and neatly whenever possible.* You must realise that when you wear smart clothes, your emotions tend to be affected positively, which in turn raises your overall vibration. When you are well dressed you are likely to feel more confident and at ease. Using a good "packaging" will generally affect your thoughts in a positive way. Besides, when you look smart, you are likely to make a better impression on others; you will look more dependable and likeable. Cialdini states that people tend to naturally assign additional qualities to likeable people, such as generosity, kindness and intelligence, without even knowing if they are true.

*Always have a relaxed posture.* Excessive tension in your body presses on your organs and makes your respiration more difficult. In order to have an erect posture, imagine that in the top of your head you have a cord that pulls you upwards and stretches your spine. You can also imagine that your bones are like a scaffolding structure that sustains your flesh. The frequent use of these techniques will make your muscles relax almost instantaneously. Remember that a relaxed state generates high vibrations, which in turn accelerates the manifestation of your dreams.

*Do organic movements.* You can try to make your movements more organic, feeling that your energy comes from your abdomen and radiates to the rest of your body. Some disciplines like yoga may also improve your posture. The use of your abdominal respiration (explained in the chapter about meditation) tones your vessels and muscle groups and induces you into a state of energetic calmness.

*Laugh whenever possible.* There are many studies that certify that laughter improves your capability to reflect on problematic situations. When you are in a good mood you can deal with troublesome situations more efficiently. It is also a natural way to release tensions and stay relaxed. Laughing raises your energetic vibrations, with all the benefits related to this.

## 5.2. Gestures

In your daily activities, the use of energetic gestures affects your thought and emotions in a positive manner. You should always act confidently, as if your physical actions precede your emotions. Always use lively gestures; they will bring about good feelings. Your face gestures also affect your mood and thoughts.

Try to smile at all people you meet, even strangers. Many research studies certify that smiling, even in a fake manner, tends to modify your overall emotional state positively. You should get accustomed to smiling whenever possible; you will radiate more positive energy.

It's important that you also smile with your eyes and body. Visualise that you have a smile in each eye. Also envision that you have thousands of smiles all over your skin. This technique will affect your energy positively, raising it.

## 5.3. Vocabulary

*If we listen to the words of failure multitude we will soon learn that by their words they are justified and condemned.*
*Julia Seton*

The use of positive vocabulary also affects your emotions and thoughts, which in turn shifts the energy you radiate. If you are accustomed to using poverty vocabulary you will attract more financial difficulties to your life over time.

Some examples of restrictive words which should be completely eradicated from your vocabulary are: problems, needs, impossible, limitations, greed, lack, competition and strife, among others. On the contrary, the use of uplifting terms such as *"I am"*,*"* I *choose", "I decide"* or*" I am able"* generate good vibrations and hasten the manifestation of your dreams.

You should be very selective with the words that you use in your daily conversations, with other people and yourself. Be aware that words, in fact, shape and define your circumstances. Words are the expressions of your thoughts, the reflection of your belief system.

The terms you use frequently help you interpret your experiences in your particular way. If you get accustomed to using positive vocabulary, you will see your circumstances, even the negative ones, in a better light. As a consequence you will raise your overall vibration, which will make you attract good things to your life.

In conclusion, try always to use positive, expansive and empowering terms. For example, don't talk about *"problems that you have"* but *"challenges to overcome"*. Besides,always use a loud and clear tone of voice. This will give you much more enthusiastic clout, which will raise your energy levels.

# Chapter 9

# Setting Goals

*If you want to be rich, your goal has to be rich.*
*T. Harv Eker*

## 1. Importance of goal-setting process

When you set goals you are harnessing your infinite power. You are not only strategising, you are earnestly committing to achieving your dreams. In this way, goal setting is a powerful way of motivating yourself and staying in a positive mood. From the metaphysical perspective setting goals is a very important tool to achieve prosperity. When you set goals you are communicating your dreams to the Universe in a very explicit and overt manner.

To put this simply, when you set goals, you are actually indicating to the Universe what you want. So your goals must always be stated as end results. This means that you should never state how those goals will be attained. The "how" is the domain of the universal forces, not yours. For example, your goal can be *"I deserve to have £1,000,000 in one year's time"* You should not be stating how you will get this money, rely on the Universe's wisdom. The universal forces will find the best way and resources for the materialisation of your desires. Instead, if you state the means by which those goals will be achieved, you are actually hindering the Universe's limitlessness. This attitude will delay the manifestation of your desires.

You may begin asking yourself some questions about your general goals regarding prosperity. In that effect, ask yourself questions *"What are the underlying reasons to become prosperous?"* or *"Why do I want to be rich?"* When you answer these questions, try not to focus only on money. Instead, relate your answers to the feelings you want to experience with prosperity. For example *"I want to be rich because I want to feel safe... recognised... loved... admired"* It's important to highlight that there are always hidden emotions behind the objective of obtaining more money. Try to find out more about these feelings in order to explore them in detail.

Setting goals is a way of crystallising your innermost desires. For this reason, it's advisable to write down your goals, instead of holding them as thoughts in your mind. By writing your goals down, you make them more solid and tangible. You can also re-read them whenever you want.

Your objectives can also be stated as empowering affirmations. The techniques for affirmations will be explained later in this book. For example your goals can be worded using expressions such as *"I allow myself to... "*. You can simply use *"My objectives are..."*. At the beginning, you should try to write down as many aims as possible. Later you can re-read the list to refine it and narrow down the amount.

Try to not to use the wording *"I want..."*, because the term *"want"* implicitly entails scarcity, something that you don't have. Instead, use words such as *"I choose..."*, *"I deserve to have..."* or *"I am on my way to having..."* among others.

## 2. Tips to set goals effectively

### a) Goals as guidelines

The goals represent cornerstones or guidance for your plan to manifest your dreams. They are the oxygen of your strategy; it cannot survive without them. Goals are the compass of your life ship. Without goals, your life will be a constant improvisation, and you'll be reacting only to whatever comes to you.

It's possible that, in some cases, you don't feel comfortable setting goals because of hesitation, indecisiveness or lack of merit. If this happens to you, ask yourself this question: *"What are the actual costs of not setting any goals?"* By answering it wholeheartedly you feel more encouraged to set objectives.

Setting goals is like sowing the seeds in an agriculture activity. You need to select the right seeds (setting the right objectives). Then sow them in good soil (your tranquil focused mind and positive emotions) for the crop to be successful. Besides, these seeds should be cared for. You care for your objectives by reading them frequently. You also take care of them by not commenting to anybody about them (secretiveness). You protect them by taking appropriate action whenever necessary.

### b) Making a list

Setting goals is a very relevant activity to increase your prosperity. As it was said goals are the main factor of any plan or strategy. There is a very well-known saying that goes *"If you don't know where to go, you will end up anywhere"*. By writing down your aims, you set the direction that you want to go in. From the metaphysical perspective, the goal-setting process helps to channel the universal energy in a specific direction.

A very simple exercise is making a list of specific goals about money. When you write down the list try to be quite thorough regarding the details, but not too much. When you write down the goals, try also to feel relaxed. If you feel tense, you can practise meditation first, and then describe your objectives.

Try to write your objectives when you are in a good mood. You should always pay attention to your feelings when you write down the goals. Take note of any negative emotions or thoughts arising when you write the goals. Acknowledge those negative feelings, accept them and release them. In the case of thoughts, replace them for more positive ones.

You can also keep an updated record of your goal in a computer or in a notebook. Remember to read these goals on a daily basis. This discipline will help you attract the resources for the achievement of your aims more quickly. After the list of your goals you can include your signature to pervade them with your unique empowering energy.

## c) Intention and commitment

When you set your objectives, it's imperative to support them with unwavering intention. From a metaphysical perspective, intention is the most powerful energy that you deal with; it helps you achieve your goals.

To put it simply, your goals are *"what you want to do"* and *"where you want to go"*. Your intention is *"why you want that"*. So when you set goals, ask yourself about the intention underneath the goals. *"What is the main purpose of setting this goal?"* or *"Why do I want to achieve this goal?"* By answering these questions, you will get some fruitful insights about the main feelings propelling each goal. Take note of the main motivators behind each goal.

The motivation to achieve goals is always about specific emotions. For example, you may want to have £1,000,000 because you want to feel safer and more confident.

Besides, it is also important to be committed to the goals you have set. In some cases, fulfilling your objectives could take much more time than expected. However, this is not a reason for abandoning your goals.

## d) Visualisation

Anthony says visualising is like playing in advance a specific scenario in your mind. This author states that *"by using visualisation to see your goal in a complete manner, you will eliminate or certainly reduce the stress of trying to achieve something you wouldn't ordinarily believe can be yours"*.

For the above reason, it is of value to visualise the achievement of the goals. When you visualise you are mentally rehearsing the achievement of your objectives. In that effect, your goals can be reflected as a part of the collage in your treasure map or vision board.

When you visualise your goals, you should include all the

emotions and sensations you imagine you will experience when you attain them. By including vivid images and intense feelings in relation to your aims, you are accelerating their attainment. It is important to feel the objective as if it were achieved. The objectives can also be enriched by using other specific sensations such as touch, smell, sound, etc. All other details about visualisation techniques were explained in a previous chapter of this book.

### e) Positive wording

Your goals should be definite and positive. For example, *"having money"* is a very general goal, too abstract and not definite. *"Having £1,000,000"* is a more specific objective. You can also set the time in which you want to have the money for example "by..." As it was explained before, you don't have to include in the objective the way by which it will be achieved (for example don't include *"...as a consequence of winning the lottery")*.

The objective *"Not being poor"* is another example of an erroneous goal, because it is not stated in a positive manner and besides it's too general. For this reason, when you set the goal, you should always focus on what you want (and not on what you don't desire).

When you use positive wording for your goals you are energising them with high vibrations. There are other ways of energising your objectives. In that sense, Nemeth says that you can energise your goals by spending money and time on them, rejoicing about them and obtaining support from people.

However one of the most important things for the success of your goals is spending time focusing on them. In that sense, you must concentrate on your objectives frequently and with undivided attention. Find below other traits of ideal objectives.

*Meaningfulness:* This means that the goal is important to you. Your goals must be directly or indirectly related to what you love to do. From a wider perspective they must be linked with your specific mission in life.

*Attainability:* From the metaphysical viewpoint you can achieve any objective. However at the beginning you should set objectives that are realistic and credible, in order to gain confidence in the manifestation process. For this reason, try to make your goals sensible while you get used to this idea. If you have been earning £1,000 a year, setting an objective of £1,000,000 may be a bit too much from the outset.

*Fun:* Your goal is not an obligation or a chore to you; on the contrary, it is something pleasurable for you.

I*ntegrity*: Your objective should be morally correct. You don't want to achieve at the expense of others, you don't want to manipulate other people either. The following is an example of an objective lacking integrity: *"I want to have £1,000,000 from Mr. John's possessions".*

## f) Related to your innermost desires

From the metaphysical perspective, each time you set an authentic goal, a burning desire of yours is activated energetically. In that effect, you should only write goals that are heartfelt, those that you truly want. The main point of reference when you write goals is your heart, not your mind.

The objectives you set must be motivating, inspiring and expansive for your life. You should never set mediocre goals. On the contrary, always set ambitious objectives; think big, you are a limitless being. You must also feel worthy of achieving those goals. Be aware that setting valuable objectives may imply leaving your comfort zone. Setting high goals tends to improve your self-image.

Some questions that you can also ask yourself are *"What are my main objectives to have the perfect life?"* or *"What is the specific amount of money that I want to obtain?"* This type of question helps you with the goal-setting process.

You can ask yourself *"Do I feel any resistance regarding this goal?"* If so release the negative emotions, using any of the methods explained in this book such as Sedona, tapping system, visualisation, affirmations, meditation, among others.

Don't include aims that you feel you are constrained by or obligated to achieve. You should never set goals that others want you to achieve, for example your family or friends. Be aware of social conditioning exerting pressure on you. You should set goals that are essential to you, unless you actually agree with the advice given by other people on this.

### g) Realistic perspective

This aspect has to do with the attainability and credibility of the objectives you set. In that sense, your goals must be feasible and realistic; you must believe that you can achieve them. However remember that when you set objectives you have the support of the almighty universal forces which will assist you. For this reason, don't be conservative.

From the metaphysical perspective, you can achieve any objective you want, even the ones that appear totally unattainable to you, However, the purpose of setting viable goals, at least at the beginning, is to gradually strengthen your faith in you and the universal forces. Over time, you can set higher objectives, the objectives that in the past you considered totally "out of your league". For this reason, it is advisable to begin testing with small objectives, and then go through to bigger goals.

Another point to analyse is the case of multiple objectives. If you have too many goals there are some criteria you can use to screen the most valuable ones. For example, have a look at the ones that seem more pleasant. Ask yourself *"Which of these goals would bring me more fulfilment?"* and give special priority to them. Another criterion is the connection of the goal with your strengths and passions. In that sense you should always select the objectives that make you more worthy, the ones that you can apply your skills to and those that you feel more passionate about.

If you actually set more than one objective, you should appraise them carefully. Check if they are compatible with one another. Also verify if the goals can be attained simultaneously, or some of them must be accomplished first.

In some cases, it is possible to break down your objectives, divide them into smaller objectives, called sub-objectives. This is very common when your goals look too big or far away in the future. In that case, you can give priority to the sub-objectives that should be attained first, to later focus on the successive ones.

## h) Flexibility

You should be flexible regarding your goals. In that sense, your objectives can always be modified over time. In some cases, you might have discovered your most authentic goals, through a process of trial and error. It's also possible that you might have realised that the goals you set before are not of value for you anymore. In this case, you can replace or update your aims.

It was explained that you can also set deadlines for your objectives. However, over time, you must also discover that you must be flexible with the time of achievement of your aims. An objective that might have been apparently easy to achieve is actually more challenging than expected.

## i) Secretiveness

Another point to highlight is secretiveness. In that sense, when you set goals, you should always keep them secret. Don't tell anybody about them, unless they are extremely trustworthy and supportive. It's important to keep your aims secret because when you tell anybody about goals, you are dispelling the energy that empowers them. As a consequence, this may delay or hinder their achievement.

There is a second reason for you to be secretive about your objectives. If you tell people that are not supportive about your objectives, before you attain them they may criticise you. Some people tend to be jealous of others, if you tell them about your aims, they may make snide remarks about your goal. These types of comments radiate negative energy, which may hinder the manifestation of your desires.

### J) Different timelines and areas

You can write down goals regarding different timeframes (next week, next month, next year, etc.). You can also include goals in relation to different areas (prosperity, health, relationships, etc.). Setting objectives doesn't have to be limited to wealth creation.

Start writing down goals that are simple to achieve, then continue with goals that are more complex. However, as it was explained previously, from the perspective of the universal forces, there are no difficult objectives. From the universal perspective all goals are equally achievable; it is your mind that imagines potential difficulties.

### k) Receptivity

Once you set your goal you should be in a receptive position. Every person has a masculine polarity and a feminine polarity. Receptivity entails the application of the feminine polarity. From the metaphysical perspective, this polarity is also related to these others traits: fertility, creativity, association, effortlessness, affection and sensitivity. In that sense, the feminine polarity is opposite to any competitive, pushy and effortful action. In other words, by being receptive you allow your desires to come into your life without any resistance. You don't have to make any effort either, because you are fertile by nature.

In order to tune in with your feminine polarity, once you set your goals, imagine yourself actively listening to a person when you hold a conversation. Visualise that you will give close and full attention to the speaker without interrupting or judging him or her. In that state, you are being totally receptive.

The same analogy applies to your goals. After you set them

you should remain relaxed and receptive, attentive to the universal messages. You can continue focusing on the goals regularly. However you should not judge how your goals will manifest, only pay attention to the signals that will appear over time. Try to be faithful and serene; don't rush, and don't get desperate. Allow things to evolve in their own way. Cast away any negative thought or emotion. And try to avoid taking thoughtless or reckless actions to pursue your goals.

## l) Gratefulness

When you have achieved any of your goals, you should be grateful for this. You should always celebrate the achievement of your aims cheerfully. An example of this, you can reward yourself with gifts, or have dinner out. The main aspects of celebration were explained in the chapter of gratitude.

It is advisable to have a journal of your achievements and read it regularly. By keeping an updated record you will attract more accomplishments. However, bear in mind that achieving the goal should be as important as enjoying the process. If you are upset during the process of achieving your goals and you are only happy with the accomplishment, your objectives might not be authentically fulfilling.

## Goals and actions

Setting goals does not mean waiting for achievements without taking any action. Sometimes you may take action in relation to your objectives. However, all actions that you take must be authentic and inspired. In that sense thoughtless or automatic actions are unlikely to help you attain your aims. This type of action radiates negative energy, which hinders the manifestation of your desires.

Uninspired actions tend to be effortful or extremely demanding. They are not heartfelt; you don't feel completely at ease when you perform them. In fact, these actions deplete your vital energy. In short, these actions may be of very little use for the attainment of your goals. Remember the universe always works effortlessly, so apply this fundamental principle to your actions.

Each time you take authentic actions, you are reinforcing your intention. Inspired actions re-energise your goals. When you take this type of action you feel connected to the Universe, and in a state of flow. The state of flow is explained in one of the appendices.

When you are taking actions in an inspired manner, you implicitly confirm to the universe that you are still committed to the achievement of your desires. By taking inspired actions you show the universal forces that your objectives are not temporary whims, but instead, earnest wishes.

If you have doubt about the actions to take, ask yourself *"What is the obvious and easiest step I feel I can take right now?"* Wait for any insight about this. The Universe tends to give precious insights. You can receive intuitive signals about how to act. The main aspects of intuition will be explained later in this book.

After you take the first step ask for the next obvious step, and so on. In order to attain your goals you should follow a stepwise and expansive process. In some cases, small actions, also called baby steps are OK. Never ever try too hard to achieve your goal; that will easily deplete your energy. Trying hard does not work because it is generally based on anxiety, anguish, fear or desperation, all bad feelings. All these emotional states radiate negative vibrations, which push away the materialisation of your dreams.

your chakras. Reiki is also good for this.

Below you will find several well-known methods to cleanse the chakras. You can use these tools on your own. These techniques will help you clear up the energetic pathways and eliminate their negative patterns. Some signals that show that your chakras are blocked are excessive tiredness or overexcitement. You should look carefully at the moments when you don't feel in balance. In those cases you should accept the existence of blockages in your energy system in order to purify it willingly.

When you use the following exercises to cleanse your chakras some emotions might come up; try not to suppress them, let them arise naturally. You should welcome any feeling that appears, in order to release it effortlessly.

Some benefits of cleansing your chakras:

*Your overall vibration will be raised.* You will feel more at ease, more energetic and, in general, healthier.

*You will let go of any resisting energy.* By cleansing your energetic centres you banish all hindrances regarding the manifestation of prosperity in your life.

## A) Contact with nature

Several authors like Sharomon, Bodo and Baginsky suggest a method to cleanse the chakras that involves getting in contact with natural elements. This widespread technique is simple, easy to use and very effective.

For example, your first chakra can be harmonised by being in contact with nature; more specifically you should sit on the floor. You can also stand bare foot on the floor, preferably lawn or sand.

In order to equilibrate your second chakra it is advisable to contemplate natural watery landscapes such as rivers, sea, etc. To clear up the third chakra you should stare at sunny sceneries.

In order to balance the fourth chakra, you should get in contact with red natural elements, for example you should observe red flowers or a reddish sky. To clear up the fifth chakra, you should look at the blue sky.

You can purify the sixth chakra. In order to do so, it is advisable to look at the sky, especially when it is thronged with stars. In order to open your seventh chakra you can go to places which are close to the sky. For example, you can climb a mountain.

## B) Beam of light

A very effective technique to clean the chakras is to imagine a ray of violet light coming into your body from the top of your head, and then going down your neck, all over your spine, until the coccyx. Then visualise the ray going up from the coccyx to the top of your head throughout your spine.

In some cases you can extend the beam of light beyond the coccyx, towards the soles of your feet. Then visualise it going upwards from your feet towards the head. You can repeat this exercise as many times as you want. The beam of light can be a golden colour.

There is a variation on this cleansing practise. You should imagine the sunlight above your head. See the light going down from your head through your spine to its lower part, and then going upwards. When the ray reaches your throat imagine it dividing into three rays; two of them going through each arm and the third going up through your head again.

There is a third variation of this technique. You imagine a beam of light coming into the crown chakra, going down and irradiating light outwards from the solar plexus chakra.

There is a fourth way of applying this technique. You imagine being surrounded by a circle, oval or a pyramid of golden or pink light. Visualize that it pervades all the chakras cleansing them.

Another well-known variation of this technique is to imagine the radiant beam of light spiralling up around your spine while cleansing all the chakras one by one, from root chakra to the crown chakra. Then you must imagine the same beam of light spiralling down around your spine, from the crown chakra to the root chakra. This light cleanses each chakra, one by one.

## C) Breathing through the chakras

There is another interesting tool to cleanse your chakras. You must imagine that you breathe in and out from each chakra. Start breathing in and out through the first chakra, and then the others, but one at a time. You can also start, instead, with the chakra at the top of your head and then continue with the rest.

By breathing consciously through the different chakras you will harmonise them effortlessly. You must locate your consciousness on the specific chakra that you are dealing with, and dismiss the rest. The breathing rhythm could be slow and light, or quick and intense.

In each chakra you should visualise the air going in and out. You must visualise breathing in and out from the front and back parts of each chakra. However the crown chakra only opens upwards, so you will only breathe from that part. The root chakra only opens downwards, so you will only respire from that part.

To make this exercise easy, you can imagine that in each chakra there is a pipe, which is filled with air and emptied up. You can also imagine that there are "lungs" on each chakra, which are filled and emptied with your breathing.

Another way to cleanse chakras is to visualise inhaling the energy of Earth coming through the soles of your feet. This energy goes upwards throughout your spine cleansing each energetic centre, one by one. When you visualise this, you should feel love and thankfulness.

## D) Different coloured beams of light

You can visualise a specific coloured light bathing each chakra. From the metaphysical perspective, each energetic centre is related to a specific colour that identifies it distinctively.

For your first chakra (root chakra) you should imagine a red beam of light. For your second chakra (sacral chakra), try to visualise a light orange ray. For your third centre (solar chakra) you must imagine it pervaded by a golden ray.

You should imagine a pink ball of light with green borders pervading your fourth chakra (heart chakra). Your fifth chakra (larynx chakra) must be impregnated with a light blue ray. The sixth, (third eye) must be bathed with a dark blue beam of light with copper-coloured twinkling. Finally the seventh centre (crown chakra) must be pervaded with a ray that is golden with violet.

# Chapter 11
# Feng Shui

## 1. General aspects

*When we live in harmony with all living things, our lives progress more smoothly and we find it easier to achieve our goals... how we arrange each room in our home can make an enormous difference to the quality of our lives.*
*Richard Webster*

Feng Shui is the art of creating a harmonious relationship between you and your environment. From this perspective, you are always influencing your environment and vice versa; everything is interconnected. Your place is one of your main ways of expressing and sensing. Every detail of your place has a meaning and an energetic charge, which can be positive or negative. This millenary discipline deals with five elements: wood, metal, water, earth, and fire. In that sense, water is the symbol of economic abundance.

This discipline is based on the principle that everything is energy. From this perspective, everything is pervaded by the vital energy called *chi*. This energy vibrates, even in the case of things that look still. Abundance has its own vibrating field. Your place should correspond to the abundance vibration if you want prosperity in your life.

In that sense, you can purposefully create an abounding flow in every area of your life. To do so, the vital energy (called chi) should circulate freely in every area of your environment. When this energy chi is circulating restrainedly in your place, you are likely to have financial difficulties. For example you can get into debt or you may lack money.

On the contrary, when that energy flows in an unhampered manner you are likely to have a prosperous financial situation. To put it simply, constricted flow of energy causes damage to your financial position.

For this reason, if you want to be more prosperous, you should purposefully set up good vibrations in your environment. When the energy circulates unrestrainedly in your place, copious amounts of money are likely to manifest in your life.

## 2. Feng Shui tips to attract abundance

These Feng Shui techniques will help you eliminate any blockage or obstacle obstructing your place. In this section the basic aspects of this discipline will be explained. For further knowledge, you should see specific books cited in the bibliography. Find below some tips to take into account.

It is important that you check that the vital energy (chi) flows effortlessly inside your house or your workplace. Look for places where the energy stagnates. In those places you will sense that the energy is heavy, stuffy and dark. Look also for places where clutter is accumulated and get rid of the unused or worthless stuff. In that sense, Robert says that *"...clutter blocks your sources of abundance and makes it hard to nourish yourself and others. De-cluttering... opens up space for you to receive the financial and emotional nourishment that you need in life."* The de-cluttering techniques were explained in a previous chapter.

Abundance is one of the nine sectors you can divide your place into. It's important that you locate the richness sector in your place according to a Feng Shui perspective. In order to do so, you must stand up at the main entrance door of your place; the abundance area is situated in the left corner at the end of the house. This sector is related to money opportunities and financial success. Check that area and examine its specific energy. Look at the objects that are there. Walk around that area, put your hand on your chest and feel the energy there. Ask yourself: *"Is there clean and light energy?" "Is this area beautiful and tidy in appearance?" and "Does this area have items representing prosperity?"* If the answer to those questions is "no", try to sort that out accordingly.

You should keep all doors clear in your place. All pathways should be unobstructed. You must keep all the areas in your place well illuminated, clean and in good condition. For this reason, check that the lighting is appropriate in all rooms; avoid dark places. Besides, fix things that are broken such as doorknobs, glasses, electrical appliances or taps. You must repair or replace them as soon as possible. Taps leaking means drainage of money in your life, so fix them with no delay.

In your prosperity sector you should include some objects in yellow, gold, green and purple. These colours represent more abundance in your life. In that sector also put objects related to the water element, which represents prosperity. Some examples are an indoor fountain or an aquarium. In that sector, you can also include precious stones, crystals, priced objects, seeds and acorns, art items, or plants with rounded leaves. In the prosperity sector you can also put candles in light purple, gold or green. This area should be very well lit; be aware that light attracts the vital energy "*chi*".

Check each nook of your place carefully. You should discard items that are worn out, shabby or shoddy. You should also throw away any object which either you bought or received at moments you experienced bad emotions, such as fear or anger.

# Chapter 12

# Intuitive Insights

## 1. Meaning of intuition

> *Your soul's urges, the inner guidance, hunches, are concerned with something you are already familiar with directly or indirectly. These urges give you both the ideas and the momentum to carry them out.*
> *Roman Sanaya and Duane Packer*

Intuition is also called sudden discernment, gut feeling, instinct, sixth sense, epiphany, aha moment, revelation or hunches. In this book it was explained that your subconscious mind is unlimited as compared with your conscious level. In that sense, your hunches are shortcuts to your unconscious mind. The unconscious level tends to communicate through images, sounds or sensations.

The subconscious mind does not make connections in linear ways because it has an overarching view on things. In most cases, our reasoning mind cannot understand them, for example, when you have urges that push you in a specific direction. All intuitive insights have a relevant message to convey. For this reason, you should always follow your intuition, whenever possible.

When you use your intuition, you are going beyond your traditional senses, such as sight, touch, smell, hearing and taste. For this reason this inner knowing is also called "sixth sense". When you receive intuitive insights, you are not likely to be focused on your environment; instead you might be dwelling inwardly. However you don't have to make any effort to get these insights, they show up spontaneously.

Intuition is to know with no reason. This is possible because there is an infinite intelligence beyond our rational mind. That is the universal intelligence which goes beyond your ego and has the perception of the whole. When you are intuitive, you pick up messages from that limitless intelligence. These intuitive signals appear at any time, in the most unexpected ways.

According to Fiddes intuition can be made up of different signs such as physical (gut feelings, faint, whisper), emotional (tranquillity or impulse), or mental (epiphany, images). Insights can also manifest as sudden memories apparently unconnected to the moment, atypical emotions or vivid dreams. Even signs from your environment can represent intuitive insights. In some cases, the intuitive signals can be very subtle; so you have to be very attentive. All intuitive messages provide you with spontaneous insights.

Intuition is in tune with the main teachings of Metaphysics. In that sense, there is a very well-known metaphysical saying that goes *"When the student is prepared, the master will appear"* This means that when you are sufficiently receptive to the signals of the Universe or your subconscious mind, those signs will certainly appear to guide you in the best way.

The ideal states to connect with your intuitive being are silence, stillness, recreation or relaxation. However any other undisturbed or unworried state, such as glee, playfulness, exhilaration and peacefulness are suitable for intuitive insights. For example, some activities that might bring about intuitive insights are playing sports, strolling in a park, having a shower, swimming in a pool, sunbathing, among others.

Intuitive insights are guidelines for your wellbeing and inner development. Those insightful signals can be shown in different ways, such as directions to certain places, warning signs about dangerous situations, activities to carry out, people to contact, resources to obtain, among others.

For example, in the case of money, intuitive signals can tell you:

*Wise ways of investing and spending your money*
*Trustworthy people regarding money issues*
*Money activities related to your mission*
*Scam activities to avoid*
*New ways of earning money*
*Money habits that you should take up*
*Creative ways to solve your financial problems*

## 2. Different ways to improve your intuitive skills

*The intuition serves as a bridge between your conscious self and the Infinite Intelligence, the life force of all creation.*
*Dale W. Olson*

### 2.1. Asking questions

A very interesting technique you can apply is to ask questions of your subconscious mind about your money problems or any other relevant aspect in your life. After this, you should relax and wait for the answers. They are unlikely to be conveyed immediately. So keep on with your activities in an unworried way.

Over time you are likely to receive some signals, which indicate the message from your subconscious level. In some cases, the answers you receive are indirect. For example, if you ask your subconscious level "*What are other ways that I can generate money effortlessly*?" you may find a book or article that gives you the answer. You can also meet new people that advise on that issue. You may see specific images that give clues about your problem. The signals can also be sensations or voices. If you are not sure that you received the answers you were looking for, you can ask your subconscious the same question again.

### 2.2. Use of affirmations

In order to ask questions in a proper way you can use this affirmation "*Universe (or subconscious mind), show me what I have to know about..."* In case of doubt about the answer received, you can ask *"Is this my intuitive part?"* Try to be as specific as possible when you ask questions.

Try to make the questions personal, related to your life, your objectives or your mission. Your attitude after asking the questions must be of openness and receptivity. For this reason, you should never use this exercise in cases where you are strongly attached to specific results, for example, when you are eager to have things resolved in a certain way.

## 2.3. Dwelling on the issue

Some say that, after you ask your subconscious for ways to solve problematic situations, you can also continue analysing the troublesome issue from different perspectives. From this perspective, the deep examination of your issue may contribute to the reception of insightful answers from your subconscious.

However, others state that, once you ask your subconscious for a solution, you must engross yourself in your daily activities without consciously thinking about the problem any longer. The subconscious level will be elaborating the answer below the level of your awareness. This answer will be communicated to you in the most appropriate moment. From the viewpoint of this book, this second option is more adequate.

## 2.4. Answering with your non-dominant hand

In order to access your inner guidance it is also suggested that you write down the question of which you want to obtain an intuitive answer. You write that question with your dominant hand and then breathe in and out deeply. You should wait for the answer with the pen in your non-dominant hand. Write whatever comes to your mind, without any analysis of this. This is likely to be the answer to your question.

## 2.5. Asking questions of spiritual beings

When you are looking for intuitive signals, you are referring to your subconscious level, which is limitless, creative, and all-powerful. However some sages suggest that it is useful to ask your questions to your guardian angel or your spiritual supporters.

## 2.6. Traffic lights technique

There is another very well-know exercise to receive intuitive answers to your questions. This technique can be used with questions to be answered "yes" or "no". For this type of questions, you must imagine the traffic lights. You should ask the question and then see which of the traffic lights turns on.

If it is red, this means a negative answer. If the light is yellow it means "maybe"; in this case you may need more information. In the case of green, this is a positive answer. You can also use the vision of the coin. If you see heads the answer is "yes". If tails turns up the answer is "no". And in the case the coin is stood on its edge the answer is "maybe".

## 2.7. Muscle testing

Hawking suggests another technique based on kinesiology called muscle testing. In that sense he states that *"a positive stimulus provokes a strong muscle response, a negative stimulus results in demonstrable weakening of the test muscle"* This technique needs to be carried out with another person. In that technique you stand face-to-face in front of the other person, who will ask you questions about your issue.

Before the question is asked, you raise and hold your right arm, perpendicular to your torso. Then the other person will ask the question. From your wrist, this second person will try to gently pull the arm downward. When this person tries to pull your arm down, you must resist the downward pressure.

If the answer to your question is "no" your arm will go weak and, as a consequence, will be pulled down easily. On the contrary, if the answer to your question is yes, your arm will remain extended parallel to the floor, despite the downward pressure on it from the second person.

## 2.8. Use of a pendulum

Another way to communicate with your subconscious mind is to use a pendulum. Many authors, like Le Cron, suggest this tool to obtain intuitive insights. You can buy this tool in any new age shop. Instead you can use a cord with a ball or ring hung from it. Some say that this technique can also be used to predict the future. However in this book the pendulum technique will be used only to access information stored in your subconscious mind.

In order to apply this technique, you must hold the cord with your thumb and index finger, the heavy part of the pendulum must be dangling in a quiet manner. When you use the pendulum your elbow should rest on a table.

It's important to understand that a pendulum can oscillate in four ways. In that sense, the pendulum can go 1) clockwise, b) anti clockwise, c) backward and forward and d) sideways. In order to understand the meaning of these four directions, you have to ask your mind for them. There will be a specific direction that means *"yes"* and a second one that represents *"no"*. A third direction will mean *"I don't want to answer that"* and the last one *"I don't know yet"*.

In order to know the meaning of each direction, you must hold the pendulum while you ask *"Which oscillation means "yes"?* You can also think about the word "yes" intensely. The pendulum will spontaneously move in the direction that is related to that meaning (yes). Then keep on asking for the directions for the other answers, that is to say the specific oscillations for *"no"*, *"I don't know"* and *"I don't want to answer"*.

Once you know the meanings for each direction, you should

pose the question for which you want to receive insights from your subconscious mind. Then wait for the answer, it will appear with a specific oscillation of the pendulum. In case of doubt about the meaning of the answer, you should repeat the procedure. Take care that you don't move the pendulum at all; it will oscillate by itself.

## 2.9. Beam of light

There is another well known technique to receive intuitive insights called beam of light. In order to increase your intuitive skills, you must imagine yourself pervaded by a beam of light. This ray forms two aerials; the first will be situated around your head. The second aerial will be around your heart. You can imagine that the aerials will be receiving all the intuitive signals that you need.

## 2.10. Intuition awareness

Look back at your past experiences. Examine the times that you received some intuitive signals. Try to look for cases in which you followed your intuitive guidance and it ended up being correct and helpful. Try to recognise the emotions, physical tension, or temperature in your body when you received those intuitive insights in the past.

You should also review the emotions, images and sounds related to your past intuitive signals. The frequent practise of this simple exercise will make you more knowledgeable of your inner guidance. In that effect, you are to become more aware of how the subconscious mind communicates to you. As a consequence, it will be easier for you to recognise and grasp those intuitive signals when they show up in the future.

## 3. What to do with intuitive insights

When you have intuitive insights, you have to welcome them thankfully. Try not to adopt a judgemental or resisting attitude toward the intuitive revelation. Instead you should try to act on the first impression you receive. If you cannot act immediately, you should take note of the realisations in order not to forget them.

Be aware that intuitive insights are signals beyond your reasoning. In some cases the insights may appear illogical according to the parameters of your rational mind.

As a consequence, you should try to act on your intuitive insights whenever possible, avoiding procrastination. When you act based on your hunches, you take inspired actions.

Each time you take inspired actions, you will feel delighted, authentic and in total connection with your inner self. All your inspired actions tend to be carried out effortlessly. When you are inspired you cannot experience any forcefulness or tediousness. You are likely to enter the timeless state of flow, which is explained in detail in the relevant appendix.

Your inspired activities tend to be pleasant, and not a drudgery. When you carry out inspired actions, your performance will be full of contentment and clarity.

# Chapter 13

# Affirmations

*Each word is a crystallized thought.*
*William Walker Atkinson*

## 1. General aspects of affirmations

Affirmations are sentences, either spoken or written, with a positive intention. Several metaphysical masters say that affirmations are like decrees. You are decreeing what is true to you, or what you believe you deserve.

Affirmations are wonderful tools to programme your subconscious mind for the manifestation of your desires. It is very important to get used to using affirmations repeatedly. You must use them on a frequent basis to impact on your subconscious more intensely. In fact when you repeat them regularly they become part of your dominant thoughts.

It is important to pinpoint that affirmations are very efficacious instruments to use in order to bring your wishes into fruition. Each time you use affirmations you must be focused on the boundless universal supply. Be confident in the almighty non-material source that complies with all your desires.

You need to utter the sentences loud and emphatically. However you can also read the affirmations or think about them intently. In the case that you write affirmations, use highlighters to mark them in different colours. You can also accompany them with representative pictures or symbols.

When using uttered affirmations, in order to be more effective, say the sentences with authority. You must feel that you deserve what you are asserting. It is better if they can be spelled out, instead of only thinking about them. The spoken words have more intensity and power.

Some sages highlight another advantage of the spelt out affirmation. When you say your affirmations loud, they sound as if you are receiving external commands from others, which may make it easier for your mind to comply with.

It is very important to utter your affirmations, feeling the emotions of having achieved what you are affirming. These empowering sentences tend to be more effective when you are energised with positive emotions. If you feel negative emotions, it is important to leave the affirmations aside, at least temporarily.

You must never use affirmations when you are in a bad mood in order not to create any dissonance in the manifestation process. You can release your negative emotions and then carry on with the use of affirmations. Later in this book you will find some techniques to release negative feelings.

Affirmations are also motivating and magnetic statements that you can use effectively to correct your wrong beliefs. In that way, you can replace your unproductive beliefs by repeating more positive ones. With the use of affirmations you can counteract negative conditioning from your environment (family, colleagues, media, friends, etc.).

Besides, affirmations can be used to improve your self-image. In this case, you should include in the affirmation the quality you want to develop (for example *"I am wiser each time I deal with money"*). In this way you can place that trait in your subconscious mind.

Each affirmation is a seed that you plant both in your mind and the universal almighty field. With the use of affirmations you are broadcasting positive vibrations to the Universe. So you should be very careful with what you frequently affirm.

In that effect, some people are accustomed to saying things like *"The current economy is so bad"*, *"Things are too expensive"* or *"I will always be poor"* among others. What these people don't realise is that they are using affirmations in a negative way almost unwittingly. The universal forces always provide people with their request. So, in this example, the Universe will be sending these people what they affirm (or ask for), even negative things.

When you use affirmations your mindset must be of completeness, openness, abundance, receptivity, boundlessness, and interconnectedness with the Universe. You must feel as if you are a vortex that attracts everything you desire in an effortless manner.

## 2. Requirements for effective affirmations

*Affirmation is the beginning of change, the beginning of creating destiny.*
*Sandra Anne Taylor*

Find below some qualities of powerful affirmations. If you abide by these requirements your affirmations will be more effective, in relation to the materialisation of your desires.

**a) Positive and brief:** Your affirmations must be positive, so don't include the words "no" or "not". For example, don't say *"I don't want to be poor"*, instead say *"I want to be more prosperous"* It's advisable that your affirmation are worded in the present tense (*I am... I choose...*). So do not use past or future tenses. However your affirmations can also be stated in progress *("I am on the way...")*. The affirmations that you use should not be too long. In that effect, one or two lines per affirmation are enough.

**b) Personal:** This might sound obvious; your affirmations must always be related to you. So this means that, if possible, don't include any other people in your affirmations. For example, don't use affirmations like *"I am on my way to receiving £1,000,000 from Mr. Smith"*. This is an example of an erroneous affirmation because you are including Mr. Smith. In that effect, you should never use affirmations to manipulate others, because this will backfire on you. In the affirmations don't compare yourself with others. For example, *"I am richer than Mr. Smith"* is a wrong way of wording your affirmation. Bear in mind that the affirmation must only be centred on you.

**c) Repetition:** You must repeat your affirmations methodically all day long. Try to use the affirmations as much as possible. It's important to pinpoint that affirmations are not formal or idle statements. In that sense, you should never recite them in a mechanical lifeless way. On the contrary, you should say them in a lively and heartfelt manner. To put it short, never repeat affirmations like a parrot.

**d) Use of first person:** The affirmations must be stated using "I" (I am.../ I do...). However some recommend that you should use affirmations using the second person accompanied by your name (for example: You, John are...). From the metaphysical perspective, it is more advisable to use the first person "I" because it refers to your higher self.

**e) Allowing:** In your affirmations you can also use permissive terms such *"I can...", "I allow..."* or "I deserve..." But never use words that imply obligation *("I must...")*. You should not use terms that entail insecurity or tentativeness *("I will try...")* either. In order that affirmations don't sound contradictory to your belief system, you can start the affirmations with the words *"I choose"* or *"I opt for"* Besides, you should never use affirmations worded as *"I want..."* You should never use the term *"want"* because you are implicitly focusing on what you don't have, which radiates scarcity vibrations.

**f) Credible:** All affirmations must sound credible or verisimilar to you. If you find any resistance using affirmations, change their wording. Use terms that make you feel at ease. If you still feel uncomfortable, let your affirmations aside for awhile to resume with them later. You can modify your affirmations many times when you feel that the message can be expressed more accurately.

**g) Emotional:** You should always accompany the affirmations with positive emotions. In some cases you can anchor beforehand positive feelings. In order to do so, you can use the NLP techniques explained before in this book. You should trigger those emotions when you say the affirmations. Your affirmations can also include direct references to positive emotions, for example, in sentences such as *"I choose to feel ..."* Their content can also include references to your self-image for example, *"I choose to be... "*or actions *"I choose to do..."*

**h) Purposeful:** Your affirmations must be purposeful, that is to say relevant to your own life. In fact these statements can be used to improve different areas of your life, such as relationships, financial issues, health, etc. The use of affirmations related to financial issues, such as *"I am on my way to attract £1,000,000"* will contribute to your prosperity.

**i) Assertive:** Never use a pleading tone of voice or begging wording. For example, you should not use affirmations such as *"Please, Universe I wanted to ask you if you can send me £1,000,000"* In that sense, your affirmation is not a petition or a prayer. Instead, with your affirmation you are asserting what is true, what you deserve and what is about to come. When you use an affirmation you are claiming, from a perspective of deservedness, the ownership of what is yours.

**j) Focused on your desires:** in order to make your own affirmation effective, only focus on what you desire, not on what you don't want. An example of a correct affirmation *"I am on my way* *to attracting £1,000,000".* An example of an erroneous one *"I don't want to be poor"* Always listen to your inner voice; it will help you understand what you truly desire. By looking at what you don't want, you can state what you desire, using the format of an affirmation. You can transform what you don't want (for example, *"to be poor")* into an affirmation *("I am on my way to becoming prosperous").* Be aware that when you affirm the positive, the negative automatically disappears, because two opposite things cannot coexist.

**k) Effortless:** When you utter your affirmations, you should not make any mental effort. Instead you should say your affirmations calmly but firmly. If you are stressed when you use affirmations, this will be counterproductive for the manifestation of your desires. For this reason, you should be as relaxed as possible when saying your affirmations. If you feel fretful or uptight it is better not to use affirmations, until you feel more positive.

**l) Recited:** You can recite the affirmation in sync with your breathing. In that case, the first part of the affirmation should match the inhalation and the second part the exhalation. Besides, when you inhale, you can imagine being pervaded by loving energy of affluence. And when you exhale, visualise that you are radiating that energy all over your environment.

**m) Not too specific:** Don't make the affirmation too detailed, let the universe deal with the specifics. The affirmation should never be too general (such as *"I have money"*) either. However, in some cases you can use general affirmations to connect to the universe in a positive way. When you use affirmations, focus on your objectives or desires, but do not concentrate on how they will be manifested. The way your desires will materialise is the domain of the unlimited universal source.

**n) Visualised:** Your affirmations can be accompanied by visualisations; however, this is not compulsory. This technique was explained before in this book. In this case you must translate the wording of the affirmation into imagery. Affirmations can also be included in your visualisation board. Affirmations can be used in the middle of meditation. Besides you can put on music and sing the affirmations. When you use affirmations imagine that you are attuned to universal forces, which go beyond boundaries.

**o) Recorded:** Keep a record of your affirmations in a specific notebook. In that way, you can read them frequently. You should repeat your affirmations, over and over, in your spare time. Read the affirmation especially when you are queuing up, waiting for an interview, travelling by public transport, when you wake up or go to bed. Take note of any new affirmation in your notepad and read it frequently. Prepare some sticking notes with your affirmations and take them with you. You can also put them clearly in view at your house or workplace.

An example of an effective format for an affirmation is stated by Taylor. You begin the affirmation with *"I open myself to my spirit's capacity"* Then make the statement with all the things you want to receive or be. For example, you can include as an intention *"I am to be more prosperous", "I am to attract more money", "I am to be supported by people" "I am to receive and give love"*, among others.

## 3. Your attitude when using affirmation

When you use affirmation you must have a special attitude, the characteristics of which are analysed below. By having this attitude, you will be more effective regarding the manifestation of your desires.

**a) Confidence:** Trust yourself as a natural attractor. When you use affirmations for your desires expect their manifestation calmly and comfortably. In that sense, tension and fretfulness only hinder the materialisation of your dreams.

**b) Secretiveness:** Try to keep your affirmations secret. This is important because the negative remarks made by other people about your affirmations can hamper the manifestation of your desires.

**c) Congruence:** This means that, once you have used an affirmation you should never assert the opposite. This means, you must be congruent for the rest of the time, after using the affirmation. For example, if using the affirmation *"I am on my way to attracting £1,000,000"* you should not be saying contradictory things such as *"I am very poor"* or *"I cannot afford that"*. These last two statements are contradictory to your initial affirmation, which will counteract its effect.

**d) Open-mindedness and thankfulness:** It is important to include, if you wish, at the end of each affirmation *"I want this or the best possible result"* or *"With benefits for everybody involved directly or indirectly"* or *"In harmony with everybody"*. With these sentences you are giving some freedom to the universal forces to act in the most perfect way possible. Besides, you can also include the words: *"Thanks, Universe"*, *"Thanks, God"* or any similar words at the end of each affirmation. The benefits of being grateful were explained in a previous chapter of this book.

## 4. Examples of affirmations related to prosperity

Find below some examples of affirmations that you can use on a frequent basis. In that sense, you can complete the dots (...) with your desires or objectives. However you can use other affirmations made by yourself.

*I receive a waterfall of... from the Universe and I am very grateful for that. Thanks.*

*I have conscious realisation that... is coming to me, at the right time and in the perfect way.*

*I express my heartfelt gratitude for... that the almighty Universe provides me with.*

*The only all powerful provider is taking in to account all my desire of having... and it is to be delivered soon.*

*I have a wonderful lifestyle, all my desires of... are fulfilled and I am very grateful to the universal forces for that.*

*With determined intention I can see beyond appearances, to unveil the wonderful truth of... that it is waiting for me.*

*I make the right choice; in fact, I choose... this choice is in total accordance with my true heart, at all times.*

*I am an incredible being, which deserves... by birthright and all the vast inexhaustible resources of the Universe to comply with my mission.*

*I forgive everyone and myself, and release negative vibrations of grudge, hatred and resentment, and this allows me to attract...*

*I am connected to the unlimited source; I am fully connected to its gifts, and I am on my way to receiving...*

*I am willing to share my gifts with the world in an amorous way, and the world is willing to support me regarding....*

*I deserve..., and any other gifts from the Universe which always exceeds my expectations.*

*I feel intense anticipation that... is about to happen.*

*I feel comfortable because I know that... is to be fulfilled.*

*I am the victor, the conqueror of negative conditions, with the cooperation of the universe I will prosper in...*

*I trust my intuition to always make the right decisions on... the most convenient ones for me and all people involved.*

*I release any impediment that prevents me from having... I truly connect to the generous universal source that supports me in all my desires.*

*I experience joyous freedom and interconnectedness in every aspect of my life, especially in...*

*I am harmoniously and gleefully aligned with the unlimited supportive Universe that cares for all my desires and brings me...*

*I feel the flow of... coming to my life, vastly and endlessly.*

*I am seeking to receive... and the Universe is seeking to exceed my expectations.*

*I am synchronised with the universal forces that bring... for my highest purpose.*

*There is only one source of power, the inexhaustible universal supply that provides me with... copiously.*

*I am in contact with the all-powerful and ever-flowing divine forces.*

*I am growing, advancing every day, at all times, and... is coming to me.*

*My indwelling power conceives marvellous gifts for me such as.... this benefits me and all the people around.*

*With positive expectancy I believe that countless miraculous opportunities, such as... come to me, the Universe is delighted to fulfil my dreams.*

*The Universe is my loyal servant and what I desire, such as:... is brought to me effortlessly.*

*I love what I have and what I do and new blessings, such as... come to my life.*

*I am protected by the Universe and everything that happens like... is only for my good.*

*From now on I commit to following my mission every day of my life, and, as a consequence I am to attract...*

*I have prosperity in all areas of my life, especially regarding...*

*Miracles happen in my life everyday such as...*

*I am open to receive... from the Unlimited universe, because of all my inalienable rights.*

*I release the obstacles and blockages to receive...*

*I love that I am on the way to receive... and other plenteous goods provided by the almighty order.*

*My life expands and I receive... and give more at all times.*

*I am in the process of accomplishing... beyond the appearances of the current circumstances.*

*Perfect equilibrium is reigning over every area of my life, especially...*

*I intend to be the best I can be at all times, in all dimensions, for this reason I deserve...*

*I have total confidence in my capability to design my destiny according to my authentic wishes, as a consequence I am to attract...*

*I vibrate in alignment with the vital, true and expansive source, which provides me with...*

*I see myself prospering in...*

*I am a magnet that freely, effortlessly and peacefully attracts...*

*All my undertakings are governed by the Infinite Intelligence, especially...*

*I have inexhaustible endowments or resources to achieve... in a surprising way*

*I release all my limitations and I am receptive to... with ease.*

*There is a constant increase of... in my life.*

*I go beyond my past experiences and new promising conditions such as... appear in my life.*

*I know the truth that is... and it manifests in every aspect of my life.*

*I increase my income in this way... and I am very grateful for that.*

*I love myself and treat myself and others in an amorous manner and this make me attract...*

*I choose my own beliefs about money and I only select positive ones, such as...*

*I am totally capable of making others prosper and this makes me thrive too, in this way...*

*I am always in a harmonious environment that benefits the manifestation of...*

*I allow myself to accept that there is plenty for everybody, even me, and the eternal substance meets all our wishes, such as...*

*I recognise my true worth and I free myself from negative feelings and beliefs, which will make me manifest...*

*I bathe my mind, body and life with fullness and perfection of the Universe that provides me with...*

*I release my word about these desires... and, with quiet expectation I know that universal forces will fulfil these dreams.*

*I have full consciousness of my oneness with the unchanged perfection; the universal forces are to provide me with... in the best manner.*

*I am attuned to the perfect patterns of divine intervention in all things; the harmonious universal flow fulfils my desire of...*

*I am the fruitful cause of the manifestation of... and the Universe supports me.*

*My thoughts are pure, I am rich in my mind, and I am willing to receive...*

*My prosperity multiplies every day and I attract more...*

*I only allow supporting beliefs to be in my mind, such as... I am pervaded by the infinite wisdom.*

*I live in abundance; an example of this is...*

*I only act based on my limitless faith, I choose to believe that... comes to my life infallibly*

*I am pure love. My caring heart unblocks the flow that connects me to the unlimited source. I am to receive... in the most loving way.*

*I am the open door to receive... I free myself from any limitation hindering the manifestation of...*

*The sacred forces protect all my acts and guide me in all my endeavours, such as...*

*The Universe, and its omnipotent substance, is on its way to fulfil my desires of having...*

*I am a loving divine being, living in unity with all good that exists, and as a consequence I attract more...*

*I feel blessed because the universal love force is permeating my body and surroundings and brings... in to my life.*

*I can see the signals from the Universe guiding my way and act on them, the Universe shows me how to...*

*All the areas of my life are in balance and I always choose the most luminous alternatives in everything I do, I am willing to receive more...*

*The radiant, timeless and pure forces of the Universe bring me... that I deserve.*

*I am always doing the perfect work and the universal forces assist me regarding...*

*The universal forces express their power through me, and only unconditional love and glaring light permeate my life, which attracts...*

*I attract... copiously as easily as I breathe*

*I take my mind away from undesired conditions and hindrances and I am only fixated on the creative source that delivers... into my life.*

*I can feel steady betterment in my life. All things I desire such as... are coming in the best way possible.*

*I radiate only good energy to Infinity. I am in close partnership with the universal forces as an unstoppable creator of my reality, for example...*

# Chapter 14

# Emotional Release Techniques

*Never suppress feelings. You don't have to satisfy them, but don't suppress them, just let them go.*
*Lester Levinson*

## 1. Importance of emotions

As any human, you have a very important variety of emotions, each of them with different intensities. However from a metaphysical viewpoint, there are only two types of feelings: positive and negative emotions. Positive feelings naturally generate good vibrations and help you attract the objects of your desires. On the contrary, negative emotions represent resistance and push away any possible materialisation of your dreams.

It is a very well known fact that there is an interaction between emotions and rationale. Your emotions affect the way you think, and vice versa. When you experience a certain emotion you will only generate thoughts congruent with that feeling. This means that positive emotions will prompt you to have more positive thoughts.

Your feelings shape the way you perceive things. In that sense, there is a saying that goes *"your emotions colour your reality"*. When you are in a positive mood your mental acuity to approach a situation is heightened. When you experience positive emotions, you are more likely to be motivated to pursue your objectives, despite difficulties that could arise.

It was explained in this book that positive posture and vocabulary affect both emotions and thoughts in the same way. When you have a confident and relaxed gait, you are more likely to be in a good mood, as compared with a sluggish or hunched posture. When you frequently use words such as *"I can..."*, *"I choose to..."* and any other positive terms, you are likely to experience more positive emotional states, as compared with the use of terms such as *"I am lost"* or *"I am defeated"*.

It is important to pinpoint that intense negative emotions temporarily impair your discerning and reflective capabilities. In fact, negative feelings can severely interfere in your decision making process, affecting your choices detrimentally. When you are in a bad mood, you can have difficulties solving problems; you may seem to be stuck in a given situation.

All emotions, in turn, have physiological effects, for example, negative emotions like anger, cause strain and tension in your body. Positive emotions release endorphins and benefit the overall functioning of your body.

It's important to highlight that all emotions are a temporary state. In fact, emotions cannot last forever, because by essence they are *"energy in motion"*. For this reason, all emotional states tend to naturally subside after a while. However, most people hold on to emotions, especially negative feelings, more than is necessary. People tend to repress or suppress their negative feelings.

There is a subtle difference between repression and suppression of emotions, although both of them are natural psychological defence mechanisms. When you repress a threatening feeling, you unwittingly keep it on the subconscious level, denying its existence. Instead, when you suppress a negative emotion you wittingly control that feeling in a way that it is not expressed.

For this reason, it is important to be aware of your own emotions. By taking slow deep breaths and focusing your attention on your body, you are likely to recognise your feelings and their physical manifestation. In that way, you can observe your feelings as if you were a neutral spectator. After acknowledging those emotional states you can choose to release them using the techniques mentioned below.

## 2. Sedona method

### 2.1. General aspects

This simple method was originally developed by Lester Levinson. This methodology was later improved by Hale Dwoskin. In this section you will find a brief review on this tool and its application to money issues. For further details on this technique, it is important to look for specific books and seminars related to this prestigious methodology. This method teaches you how to become more aware and get rid of undesired emotions, which you may be repressing or suppressing, in order to let them go.

From this perspective, this technique is an innate skill that all people have. However most people misuse this instrument or have forgotten its existence. The frequent use of this tool is liberating, you will perform your tasks with more ease. It will also allow you to communicate with others more authentically. Other advantages of this method are having a better mood and attaining goals more effectively in your life, among others.

According to this perspective, most people react to negative emotions: 1) suppressing and repressing feelings 2) expressing them in inappropriate ways. Most people even believe that they are their feelings (for example, people tend to use statements like *"I'm depressed"* instead of using *"I feel depressed").* For the viewpoint of this method, it is important to understand that you are not your feelings. You may be holding them, tightly in some cases, but you are not them.

Holding on to negative feelings has a very important disadvantage. The feelings that you don't let go of get stuck in your system, interfering with your actions and rationale. If you have a lot of feelings that you hold on to, they will impact on your mind and body negatively. The feelings that you withhold suck your vital energy out of your system.

When you hold on to feelings, you cannot access your inner wisdom. In that sense, you tend to react or act ineffectively. On the contrary, when you do not hold emotions you are better at making decisions, and act more efficiently. You will tend to react less frequently.

This methodology states that your feelings lie to you; you have to realise that you are not your feelings. You can easily drop your feelings, in the same way as you drop a pebble that you hold in your hand. In this way you let them go, you don't hold on to them any longer.

## 2.2. Different uses of this method

### a) Basic procedure

This method has several techniques to release your feelings. The first way is letting go of your feelings. In order to do so, you can ask yourself a series of questions. First you have to picture a situation that makes you feel uncomfortable, worried or restless. For example, you can think about your negative financial circumstances, or any other issue related to money.

Then you have to welcome the images, sensations, sounds and feelings that you experience at this moment in relation to that situation. Then you should ask yourself: "Am I willing to release these feelings?", *"Would I?"* and *"When?"* The answer does not matter; you will be releasing your emotions all the same. You don't have to over analyse the answer.

After this you should imagine letting go of these emotions. In order to release your emotions you can visualise them leaving as if they were smoke floating in the air. Or you can see them as knots which are being untied. You can also visualise that you hold your negative emotions in your clenched fist and then open the fist feeling them drop away. You can also use sounds or physical sensations to represent the letting go of your feelings.

If you are doing well, you will feel lighter and more relaxed. You may also observe shifts in your energy. In some cases you may see some changes, subtle or obvious, in your actions or emotions, after the release. It's likely that you have to repeat this process many times, because some emotions were held for a long time. Every time you practise this it is like peeling an onion, you will get rid of another layer (emotion) that takes you to the centre (your inner wisdom).

According to this method, you can add other questions before you let the emotions go. *"Does this feeling come from wanting approval from others, control, security or unity with others?"* and *"Can I let this go?"* These two additional questions try to address the underlying motivators of your feelings, in order to free them.

## b) Other procedures

A second way of releasing negative feelings is to allow them to be. You can also dwell in these emotions, trying to go as deep as possible. For example if you feel desperate about your negative financial situation, don't escape from that emotion; instead dwell on it deeply. You will feel that at the beginning the emotion may get a bit more intense. But then it will subside and disappear, as if you were bursting a balloon with a pin. Even the most intense emotions are just on your surface. By nature, your core is peaceful.

Another methodology is called holistic realising. In this way you have to contrast feelings with the opposite. For example if you feel fear, you can ask yourself these questions *"Can I allow myself to be fearful?"* and then *"Can I allow myself to feel courage"*. You can also apply this to money issues with questions such as *"Can I allow myself to be poor?"* and *"Can I allow myself to be rich?"* Then you must go back and forth over these two opposite questions many times. With this exercise, the two opposite emotions tend to offset each other, and the negative one will disappear.

## c) Desire is suffering

This method is based on the principle that what you desire makes you suffer. This tenet is also stated by the Buddhist philosophy. From this perspective, wanting never equals having. If you pay close attention to this, you will realise that each time you wanted something intensely you implicitly thought that you could not have it. So from the energetic viewpoint wanting equals a vibration of lack and scarcity.

All your desires are based on lack (because you want what you don't have). This makes it more complicated to have what you crave for. When you want, your mind is focused on scarcity. From this perspective, you have to ask yourself: *"Would I rather want it or have it?"* Be open to the possibility of having, instead of wanting.

This method is helpful to let go of wanting things. As it was explained, wanting is an emotion based on scarcity. By letting go of this feeling, you will have access to your inner wisdom. In this way, you will get in contact with your powerful inner resources generally obscured by your emotions. With the release of your emotions you are more likely to achieve what you desire, as compared with the situation before the release, where you were compelled by craving.

### d) Changing

You can apply the technique explained above to your desire to change. Every time you want to change something, you have to hold on to the situation to change. In that effect; you will experience some sort of resistance, either subtle or intense.

Your desire to change generally is accompanied by thoughts that include the words *"must"*, *"should"* or *"have to"*, which trigger your resistance alarm. This makes change so difficult, most of the time. This can be applied, for example, to negative beliefs you want to change, such as *"I will always be poor"* and *"I am not capable of attracting money"*.

When you are faced with a situation of change you have to ask the questions of the basic procedure (explained in a previous point) and then let go all feelings related to the desire to change.

When you release those emotions, your resistance will be lessened. As a consequence, you are very likely to find yourself more willing to change spontaneously and effortlessly.

## e) Solving problems

The basic procedure also applies to any problem. This method encourages you to perceive problems as if they were memories. From this perspective, right now, in fact, you do not have real problems. Your problems appear to be there and to persist because you keep focusing on them. In that sense, each time you want to resolve a problem, explain it or analyse it, the difficulty appears to be more real, instead of being solved. From the metaphysical perspective there is a saying that goes *"what you focus on grows"*; In other words, you will attract more of what you pay attention to. For this reason, if you focus on the problem, despite your intention to sort it out, it will appear even more tangible.

In order to use this method, especially the basic procedure, you must word your problem in the past tense. In the example mentioned in the previous point *"I will always be poor"*, can be reworded to *"I was poor"*. In this way you can let go of wanting to solve this problem. It is important to release all the desires of solving, explaining or justifying that problem, using the basic procedure.

Your feelings of wanting to solve the problem tend to obscure your essential knowingness, which impedes you in acting effectively. By releasing the emotions related to wanting to solve the problem, you will access your inner wisdom. In this way you will count on more inner resources to face up to that situation. For this reason, it's important to let go of those feelings. The same procedures can be applied to your negative beliefs, which you can consider as specific problems.

## f) Setting goals

This method can be applied to setting goals, for example your money objectives. You should write your goals and discover the images, sensations, sounds and feelings associated with them. Then let them go in the best way. You can also explore any attachments (things you hold close) or aversions (things you push away) in relation to each objective. Then release both of them.

With this practice, you will feel freer and more capable of attaining your objectives. Each time you let go of wanting to achieve goals you regain your inner wisdom, and you can discern more clearly the best ways of attaining them.

You will also realise that you don't achieve your goals by wanting them intensely or struggling hard. Instead, you attain your objectives by letting go of the wanting of their achievement, which seems counterintuitive. When you let go of the wanting to achieve your goals, you will take action but it will be more inspired, effortless and effective. This is because your inner wisdom is not obscured by the emotions of wanting.

Lastly, from this perspective, a good way to state your goals is to use the following wording *"I allow myself to..."* In relation to money issues, for example, your objective can be *"I allow myself to have £1,000,000 in my bank account in two years' time"*. This wording can also be applied to the specific actions you must take to achieve your goals.

## g) Advantages of this method regarding money issues

Besides all the topics explained above, this method also has the following advantages in relation to money issues:

*Eliminating the fear related to the generation of more wealth in your life*
*Getting rid of attachment regarding your financial objectives*
*Releasing emotions linked to scarcity*
*Accessing your inner wisdom regarding financial issues*

*Freeing yourself from bad emotions that interfere with your financial or investment plans*
*Being more intuitive and aware of opportunities to create more wealth in your life*
*Taking actions in a more inspired and effective manner*

## 3. Heartmath techniques

*Emotions act as amplifiers of our thoughts, perceptions, and attitudes. We can have a great sound system with a state-of-the-art CD player and excellent speakers, but if the amplifier - the power source for our sound system isn't working correctly, the sounds produced by the system are severely distorted. Likewise, when our emotions - the amplifiers of our perceptions are out of balance, our view of life is distorted.*
*Childre, Martinand and Beech*

### 3.1. Main aspects

All these techniques were developed by the Heartmath Institute. For more details about this methodology, it's advisable to look for seminars and products offered by that prestigious organisation. It was said before that emotions affect your perception, discernment, and your overall energy levels. In that sense, emotional states impact on your mental and physiological aspects.

Several scientific studies have confirmed that your heart has a two-way communication with the brain, they affect each other. It's important to highlight that all your emotions, even the most subtle ones, affect your heart rate variability. According to those studies, your heart produces an electromagnetic field thousands of times bigger than the mind's. In that effect, your heart is the most powerful electromagnetic oscillator in your body. For this reason, when you focus on your heart, its rhythm tends to entrain the rest of your biological systems.

It is very common that most of your activities are carried out under the influence of your mind. You tend to worry (for example, *"I don't have enough money")* and also you judge things, people or yourself *("I'm not capable of becoming rich").* In that sense, your mind has the natural tendency to categorise facts on a frequent basis. In some cases, your rationale may be ineffective, especially when you get entangled with over analytical approaches to situations.

On the contrary, when you are primarily focused on your heart, you tend to be intuitive and creative. The solution to your problems is likely to be holistic and integrative. In that sense, when you concentrate on your heart, you can access the core aspects of problematic situations, without becoming embroiled in a volley of expectations and assumptions.

When you focus on your heart, your thoughts become more lucid naturally. With your concentration on your heart, your perception of things is more intuitive. In that sense, *Childre, Martinand and Beech state that "the heart links us to a higher intelligence where spirit and humanness merge... The heart is not mushy or sentimental"*

## 3.2. Techniques

### 3.2.1. General description

You will find below a brief review on the main techniques developed by the Heartmath Institute and their applications to money issues. These tools will help you release negative emotional states regarding money (such as fear, guilt, etc.). With the frequent application of these techniques you will also be more focused on your love energy. This will help you eliminate the blocks that hinder your way to prosperity. At the same time you will develop wiser and more authentic solutions to your financial problems. In that sense, your heart will act as an intuitive guide to approaching any issue related to money and any other issue.

According to the Heartmath Institute, each time you focus on your heart, you are inducing yourself into a state of coherence. In that state, your heart rate tends to be more balanced. At the same time your heart develops a more supportive alliance with your mind; both are synchronised and work harmoniously. In a coherent state, your perception becomes clearer. Your effectiveness also tends to increase and your communicational skills become more enhanced. In a state of coherence you access your inner resources tending to be more creative and your work effortless.

It's important to know that, from this perspective, negative emotional states (such as fear, guilt) reduce your coherence; instead, positive states such as appreciation, forgiveness, and compassion increase it, with all its positive effects. All the tools explained below are learnable skills. It takes some time to master them, but in all cases their benefits are unlimited.

### 3.2.2. Freeze-frame Technique

This tool can be used when you are in a negative emotional state (for example, if you feel desperate because of your financial problems). In that situation, you must freeze your perception on the negative circumstances. In order to do so, you should imagine that you pause a video player. Visualise temporarily suspending that situation (as if it was a "movie") in a specific frame.

Then shift your attention from your head to the area of your heart. In order to do so, visualise breathing in and out from your heart. Try to remember a past experience, where you were experiencing good feelings like appreciation, compassion or forgiveness. In the example given before, you can recall experiences where you received money and you were grateful. Evoke those emotions and feel them in the area of your heart.

After that, ask your heart for guidance about the troublesome situation and then wait for its answer (in the previous example you can ask *"How can I solve this financial problem?"*). You may receive some insights at that moment or later. This technique will help you shift your emotional state (in the example, from desperation to gratefulness). By purposely focusing on your heart, your heart rate is induced into a state of equilibrium. You can also access creative insights to solve the problematic situation more effectively.

### 3.2.3. Cut-thru technique

This second tool is very useful to tackle intense detrimental emotions or longstanding ones. This technique will help you dissolve your emotional blockages. An example of this can be longstanding resentment towards people in the past that made you lose money. First of all, you must identify your disturbing emotional state. Then shift your attention to the areas of your heart and solar plexus. See yourself respiring appreciation and love energy in those areas.

Then imagine that you perceive the negative emotion from an outsider's viewpoint (as if you were a neutral beholder). You should see the situation in a totally detached manner. This will help you become less reactive. After this, concentrate on your rational heart. In that sense, try to perceive the situation, as objectively as possible, not by using your mind but your mature heart. Visualise bathing your negative feelings with compassion dissolving their relevance in your life.

Finally, ask your heart for advice and wait for its answer. You can also dwell on a state of appreciation, which tends to accelerate the delivery of your heart's answer.

### 3.2.4. Locked-in technique

This technique helps develop a better relationship with your heart. It also replenishes your vital energy. Besides this tool helps you calm down and be less reactive to negative circumstances. It can also provide you with inspiring insights.

You should be in a comfortable and silent place. Then shift

your attention from your head to the area of your heart and visualise respiring in that area. In order to do so, evoke moments in which you experienced love, appreciation, or any other positive emotional state, for example a moment in which you felt happy because of having received money. You should dwell on these positive feelings as long as you want. After this radiate these emotions to your environment. You can visualise the positive feelings reaching all people and objects in your surroundings. After this, ask for inspiring insights and wait for the answer.

If when applying this tool, your focus tends to go back to your head, you should gently switch it to your heart area. If during that exercise, you experience feelings that are too intense, you must try to relax and visualise softness in the area of your heart.

### 3.2.5. Energy assessment

There is a fourth technique that is very simple but also effective. From the energetic viewpoint, your negative thoughts and emotional states (called energy deficits) such as fear, guilt and worry deplete the energy of your body. On the contrary, positive thoughts and emotions, which are called energy assets, replenish your energy levels and, in turn, improve your overall performance. As it was explained, some examples of positive emotional states are appreciation and forgiveness.

For this reason, it's advisable to keep a journal of the different thoughts and feelings that increase and decrease your energy. By being aware of these energy generators and wasters you can take inspired action to achieve a positive balance (energy gain). For example, you can eradicate detrimental energy expenditure (complaints about money, resentment to rich people, etc.) and engage in more energy generators (positive expectancy about your financial situation, appreciation for the things that you have).

All the techniques used in this method are in accordance with the metaphysical viewpoint on emotions. In that effect, all negative emotions radiate low vibrations, which push away the manifestation of your desires. On the contrary, good feelings radiate high quality vibrations, which accelerate the materialisation of your dreams. In that sense, Childre, Martinand and Beech state that *"the emotional resonance you send out from your coherent heart rhythms is like a magnet, attracting people, situations, and opportunities"*.

## 4. Tapping system
### 4.1. General description

This method is also called Emotional Freedom Technique (EFT). Like acupuncture, EFT deals with the energy that runs over different channels crossing all over your body, which are called meridians. The tapping system is based on the premise that negative feelings cause severe disruptions in your body energy. So by tapping on specific points, in a certain sequence, you can restore your energy balance.

With the use of the tapping system, you will be able to release negative feelings and focus on positive ones. The frequent application of this method will help you to restore your overall equilibrium. This method can help you free yourself from any negative emotions, putting you in a more positive state. After practising this, you feel noticeably relieved and self-centred. Some state that this tool can also be used to modify the recording played by your inner critic.

EFT is a quick, smooth and simple technique to release undesired emotions. This discipline does not have any side effects. It is actually very easy to apply to you or other people. With the application of this technique you easily improve your mood. As a consequence, you will raise your vibration dramatically. In this way you will be in a more powerful position to manifest your desires.

## 4.2. Different steps to apply this method

In order to apply the tapping system you must go through the following steps:

### a) Recognise your problem

First of all, you have to assess your problem thoroughly. To do so, it is important that you rate your problem. You assign to your problem a level of difficulty from one to ten, ten being the hardest and one the least severe. To measure this you use your own judgement.

Let's suppose that you have economic difficulties, so word your problem as *"I have little money and feel poor"*. Rate this problem from one to ten. Try also to include the feelings related to your problem, whenever possible. You should be prepared to accept your current feelings; it's important not to resist them.

### b) Prepare a set-up statement

This is a sentence that you will repeat when you tap on specific points of your body in a sequence. In the example of the problem mentioned before, the set-up statement could be *"Even though I have little money and I feel poor, I completely and deeply accept myself"*.

As you can see, this sentence has two parts. The first one *"Even though"* is accompanied by a brief description of your problem and associated feelings. In the second part *"I completely..."* you are stating that you accept yourself, regardless of your difficulties.

Acceptance has a very high frequency vibration. This does not mean that you are resigned to the problem. Instead, you don't put any resistance on what it is at present. This helps you release negative energy that appears when you resist a situation. You can also include in the second part other words such *"I love myself"* or *"I forgive myself"* with similar effect.

### c) Tap on your karate chop.

You need to tap on a specific point. In that sense you should tap on the karate chop. This spot is situated on the outer edge of your hand, the opposite side from the thumb. You should tap in the middle part of that outer edge.

In order to tap, you can use any hand and tap with the opposite one. When you tap on that spot, you should use the four fingertips of the opposite hand (not including the thumb). You can also use two fingers: your index finger and middle finger. You should tap three times on that spot.

The tapping must always be gentle as if you are drumming on that point. When you are tapping on the karate chop, you must spell out, at the same time, the set-up statement explained in the previous point. Repeat this three times. After this, breathe deeply to release any tension.

### d) Tap on specific points of your body

After tapping on your karate chop, tap five to seven times on each of the tapping spots indicated below These spots are on your energy meridians, through which the vital energy circulates all over your body.

When you tap on each point, you should only repeat the first part of the set-up statement, the part that refers to the problem. This is called reminder line. In the example given before, you should only say *"I have little money and I feel poor"*. You don't have to include the words *"Even though"*. You don't have to say *"I completely and deeply accept myself"* either.

While you state the reminder line, you must tap on the following points (five to seven times on each), according to the following sequence:

*The top of your head, also called crown area.*
*The spot in the middle of your eyebrow (either right or left one).*
*Outer side of the eye point (either your right eye or left one). This is*

*a spot between your eye and your temple.*
*Under your eye (either right eye or left). This point is where your eye is merged with the cheekbone.*
*Under your nose, or above your upper lip, which is the same place.*
*Below your lower lip.*
*Your collarbone, either on the left side or right side.*
*Under your arm, specifically on the side part of the ribcage. This is the point located at the same height as your nipple. You will find this point four inches below your armpit.*

You can repeat the whole sequence once to thrice, while you state the reminder line, which in the previous example was "*I have little money and I feel poor*". With the use of this sentence, you are stating your problem. At the same time, you are tuning into negative emotions related to that problem, while you tap on those points. In this way, the tapping will help you release any emotional blockage related to that problematic situation. In short, this tapping sequence will help you rebalance the overall energy in your body.

After completing the sequences, you should take a deep breath. You will probably feel more relaxed and lighter. Also check how you feel about your problem now, according to your subjective rating. In that sense, try to rate your problem again, from one to ten. It's very likely that the intensity of your problem lessened.

Then you should tap on the same points following the sequence explained before. But this time you must include only positive statements. Some examples of these positive statements are:

*I am feeling thankful for...*
*I feel gratitude because...*
*I choose to...*
*I'm capable of...*

*I decide to...*
*I have the ability to...*
*I am open...*
*I have the ability...*
*I have faith...*
*I am achieving...*
*I become...*
*I love...*
*I am worthy*
*I am becoming...*

In those statements you must describe how you would feel, supposing that the problem was solved. In the previous example, in which the problem was *"I have little money and I feel poor"*, the positive statements can be formulated in these ways:

*"I am becoming more prosperous"*
*"I have faith in becoming more prosperous"*
*"I am open to receiving more money"*
*"I choose to be a richer person"*
*"I am worthy of receiving unlimited resources"*

You can also make your own positive statements. You have to repeat the positive statement while you tap on the tapping spots.

When you state this type of sentence you are focusing on positive feelings. As a consequence of this, your vibration becomes higher. You can also use other formats for the positive statement, such as *"I am connected to the universe"*, *"I am connecting with universal affluence"*, or *"I care for my financial freedom"*

Repeat the complete tapping sequence once to thrice, while you say the positive statement repeatedly. Then again check your emotional state, assess how you rate your problem now, on a scale of one to ten. Ask yourself *"Did the problem diminish in its intensity?"* If so, take a deep breath. If not, keep tapping until you feel alleviated.

You can use this technique to:

*Attract more abundance to your life*
*Be more positive regarding your goals*
*Be in a better mood to radiate higher vibrations*
*Change your beliefs and inner critique*
*Be motivated to carry out activities related to prosperity*
*Be more relaxed during the time that your desires do not manifest.*

# Chapter 15

# Playfulness

## 1. Importance of a playful attitude

*Making money is fun. Life is supposed to be fun. And millions of people are living in fear instead of having fun. That's the tragedy.*
*Donald Trump*

Playfulness is the natural essence of life. When you have a playful attitude you raise your energy levels. This, in turn, makes your desires manifest more quickly. Instead, when you take your life activities too seriously, you are constraining your energy. This, in turn hinders the materialisation of your dreams.

Playfulness is a state in which you are not offering any resistance. When you have a playful attitude, you take things as they are; you don't try to force them. Instead, you enjoy things in all their dimensions. As a consequence, when you are playful on a continuous basis you tend to face up to life events in a much easier way.

In general, many people don't allow themselves to be playful frequently. In that sense, in our society playfulness is unfairly associated with irresponsibility. Most people take their life activities too seriously, in some extreme cases like a toll, or an ordeal.

Most people tend to be overcommitted to their daily activities. They deal with them in an excessively earnest, and in some cases pushy, manner. Their activities are based on abnegation, which implies discipline, working hard, sacrificing pleasure, and making the best efforts.

For all those reasons people tend to feel distrustful of what is playful. Many people don't feel comfortable with activities that are not goal-oriented or structured. Resnick says that people have low tolerance to playful or entertaining activities. According to this perspective, people tend to act in certain ways to avoid playful activities:

*They constantly hurry up at all times, even when it is not necessary*
*They worry and feel guilty, even for insignificant things*
*They get tense and have difficulty relaxing and resting; everything is considered a chore*
*They scarcely take time to reflect on things; their minds are on automatic pilot, and their bodies are desensitised*
*They dismiss their needs; they put discipline and abnegation above fun activities*
*They act stingily or in an overprotective manner*
*They have fear of taking actions that are beyond their comfort zone*
*They act based on getting others' approval; their inner guidance is obscured*
*They are less prone to improvise and let things flow*

## 2. Playfulness and prosperity

Bear in mind that everything in the Universe works effortlessly. You should learn from nature, which always functions with ease. For example, there is no drudgery when sea waves go up and down; the planets gyrate ceaselessly with no strain. Everything in the Universe, except people, works at ease, in harmonious perfection.

For this reason, you should take things in life more light-heartedly. For example, consider your money issues less earnestly and, in turn you will be in a better state of receptivity regarding abundance. In this sense, a playful attitude regarding money is opposite to any state of anxiousness, forcefulness, worry or desperation.

All these emotional states put you in the back seat. Each time you feel upset worried or impelled to act, you are generating negative vibrations, which in turn push your dreams away. Each time that you chase money or crave for a more prosperous position you sweep those very things afar.

Instead, joy always puts you in a receptive mode for prosperity. When you are playful, you are enjoying things at present. You are absorbed in the now, with authentic enthusiasm. This uplifting energy brings about the manifestation of your desires effortlessly.

It's your choice to feel good at all times; you can decide to have a playful attitude with anything that you do. Try to make this choice everyday; as soon as you wake up. If you follow this advice, you will realise that you feel lighter; and you will also notice that things in your life flow more effortlessly.

Playfulness always raises your energy levels. By having this attitude, you attract more good things into your life. It is advisable to have this playful attitude, even when you use any of the tools explained in this book, such as affirmations or visualisation technique.

### 3. Exercises to have a playful attitude

You must consciously select activities supportive to this attitude. Choose the ones that do not drain your vital energy. Playful actions are related to joy and happiness. These activities are the opposite to states of fear and tension. Any activity that makes you feel good is adequate for this.

Feeling good is the final goal you want to achieve with all your dreams. In relation to money, you may argue and say that you want specific things, such as: buying a house, going on holiday, having a million pounds in your bank account, among others. If you analyse why you want all these things, you will conclude with no doubt, that it is to feel good.

So it is important to feel good now, even without having those things. Most people postpone their happiness until they fulfil their desires; they say that they cannot be gleeful because their dreams did not materialise.

However, from the metaphysical perspective, when you feel happy, playful and at ease now *before* fulfilling your desires (and not after achieving them), you will attract all your wishes more hastily. This happens because you radiate high vibrations, which accelerate the materialisation of your dreams.

So having a constant playful attitude and good mood is a very effective shortcut for the manifestation of your desires. It's very important that you feel good at all times. For this reason, any playful activity is supportive to this attitude. In that sense, playful activities put you in a state of excitement and lift your mood. Some examples of activities that put you in a playful state are:

*playing board games or sports*
*reading jokes on the Internet*
*attending recitals or shows*
*listening to harmonious music*
*taking a steam bath*
*having a massage*
*going shopping*
*dancing salsa*
*having holidays or a weekend break*
*reading self-help books or light novels*
*watching comedy movies*

You can also pamper yourself with any other pleasurable activity. The main criterion to follow is to participate in those activities that make you feel joyous. For example, in the case of music, you can look for classical pieces, jazz or instrumental songs. Songs with positive lyrics are suitable too. In the case of movies, romantic comedies, comedies in general and cartoon movies are very appropriate.

However, what is fun tends to very personal; this depends on the taste of each individual. The important thing to remember is that your choice should make you feel elated and relaxed. In this way you are congruently attuned with the manifestation of your desires.

Other things that can make you more playful are:

*Do things at your own pace, whenever possible. Don't rush*
*Focus on the present, and live it fully*
*Consider problems as challenges to be overcome creatively*
*Learn from children's natural playfulness*
*Evoke past moments when you were playful*
*Get in contact with people who make you feel happy*
*Schedule some specific time per day for fun activities*
*Indulge all your senses with pleasurable gifts (food, perfumes, etc.)*
*Do things related to your mission in life*
*Take some time out to relax or rest*

You can also ask yourself certain questions in relation to money issues. Some examples of these questions are *"What way of earning money will provide me with more fun?", "Which activities are more fulfilling for my mission?" "Which is the job that I would feel more joyous and authentic doing?"* and *"If I don't need to worry about money, which activities will I perform every day?"* among others. By answering these questions, you will get some interesting insights into your money issues.

On the other hand, there are some activities that are the opposite to a playful state. You have to avoid them, whenever possible. Some of them are, for example, reading the news, and in general absorbing all the negativity conveyed by the media. In that sense, most of the news is negative. For this reason, any news is likely to "pollute" your mental and emotional state. Negative events that you read in the newspaper or see on television continue to run in your mind without you noticing. They lower your mood and this, in turn, delays the materialisation of your dreams. It's obvious that other activities such as criticising, complaining and moaning are also contrary to a playful attitude.

The famous author and billionaire entrepreneur Donald Trump has a special perspective about money. In that sense, he considers that being more prosperous is like a game, in which you should have fun. He suggests that you should always enjoy the process of making more money. He also encourages people to follow their mission and only do what they love and have fun with. In fact, his vision is opposite to the perspective of struggling and fearing losing money.

# Chapter 16

# Contact with Nature

*Nature is an inexhaustible storehouse of riches; the supply will never run short... Nature is formed for the advancement of life; its impelling motive is the increase of life. For this cause, everything which can possibly minister to life is bountifully provided.*
*Wallace Wattles*

## 1. General aspects of nature

*So young our understanding. So rich our surroundings. Say less. Learn more.*
*Rumi*

Nature is the most perfect expression of pure aliveness. Each time you get in contact with natural landscapes, you are raising your energy levels. All natural scenes make you more receptive to the manifestation of your desires. In natural environments you can see nature's forces working in a smooth harmonious manner. These places are a living sample of the divine universal forces. All of these landscapes radiate positive energy, which is very infectious.

If you pay close attention to any natural landscape, you can sense the relentless but also effortless organising power underneath it. You can also realise that nature does not strive in the least; everything seems to unfold gracefully. You can apply this analogy to the creative power of your mind, which can manifest anything effortlessly. Besides, each time that you are in contact with natural places you will feel their restorative effect on your overall energy.

Find below some of the activities you should be carrying out whenever possible to be in contact with nature.

*strolling around a park*
*watching the birds flying around at any place*
*going to the river or the sea*
*exploring a forest or a wood*
*climbing a mountain*
*swimming in a creek or a lake*
*looking at the sky or a tree*
*Feeling any other element of nature such as temperature, sunshine, wind, rain, etc.*

All these activities get you in contact with the almighty universal forces. When you get in contact with the natural elements, you can realise the limitlessness of the Universe you live in.

## 2. Your attitude when you are in natural places

When you stay in a natural environment, for example a park, some activities that you can do to get most of its benefits are:

Absorb the pure energy pervading the place. Feel the stillness of that natural place filling your mind and body. Breathe unpolluted air and feel it cleansing your vital energy.

Admire the miraculous details of the landscape. Appreciate the lively and evoking colours and harmonious sounds. Dwell on the harmony of shapes, textures and materials that make up that environment. Don't try to label, judge or catalogue what you see, with rational parameters. Feel the magic of nature with all your body, but most especially with your heart area. Feel as if you were inundated by the natural crushing gorgeousness. Grasp the radiant aliveness and glorious essence of every natural element surrounding you.

Try to discover the sacredness that makes everything work in harmony in the natural environment. Feel the vividness pervading every being and thing in that natural landscape.

See how things in nature develop with ease. Look at the effortlessness that pervades the mechanics of the natural place. Try to feel synchronised with the perfect dynamics of nature. Observe how nature takes the path of least resistance with its graceful working.

Try to feel the peacefulness that reigns all over the natural environment. Feel the serenity and soothing and calming flow of nature. This will make you feel much more centred and still.

Appreciate how lavish, prospering and plentiful nature is. Observe the conspicuous abundance all over the natural landscape. Then also think about nature in general; ponder on the trillions of beings, animals and plants reproducing every second. These are self-evident examples of the opulence and limitlessness of nature. Try to relate those traits to your own creative power.

Realise that every element in nature is related to others in a synchronised manner. Feel the interconnectedness of everything in nature. Also sense your own connection with nature and all that exists. Recognise yourself as an unlimited being united with the essence of everything.

Discover that everything in nature has a purpose. This can make you aware that you also have a mission in your life. In that sense, you are an essential piece of the universal puzzle. Try to think about your purpose in life. If you don't know what your purpose is ask this question *"What is my contribution in this life?"* and wait for the answer, which may come in the most unexpected way.

It is important to mention that there are other ways to relate to nature. For example, you can talk to the natural landscape and imagine that you can hear its answers. When you are at a natural landscape, visualise that the place is filling your body, and inside of you. Some authors like Sharamon and Beginski say that *"you can also enter into direct contact with the energy of plants, however. In order to do this, sit down on the ground with your back against a tree of your liking, or embrace it in such a way that your entire body is in contact with it. Now simply permit the tree's living energy-living, harmonizing power to enter you... Plants react to your love and gratitude radiating even more energy, for it is one of their functions to help humans in this manner."*

# Chapter 17

# Energy Management

*How you manage personal energy is the new key to raising consciousness and creating a new quality of life.*
*Caroline Shola Arewa*

## 1. Energy techniques

It was commented at the beginning of this book that everything in the universe is made of energy. For example, tangible things, which are the things you can touch or see like money notes, are made up or energy. But also intangible things, like thoughts and emotions, are composed of energy. You are always in contact with different levels of energy; some of them are more dense and others lighter. You are always related to positive and negative energy.

Your vital energy can be blocked or depleted by many factors, such as negative thoughts, emotional turmoil, detrimental environments, negative circumstances, people with low energy, etc. You can also recover energy by using the different tools explained through this book such as, meditation, visualisation, affirmations, emotional releasing, among others.

Below you will find some other techniques to generate more positive energy, which in turn will attract more prosperity to your life. It's advisable to try all of these tools, at least once, to select the ones you feel more at ease with.

## 2. Absorbing

This method is called funnel technique. It is based on the principles that energy can be transferred from one object or place to others. In order to use this technique, you should imagine that you can absorb the energy from different environments or things.

For example, you can imagine inhaling the energy from luxury goods, such as expensive cars or mansions. You can also imagine absorbing the energy from trading centres or banks.

You can also walk around a prosperous area in your city and imagine that the energy of that place is pervading your whole body. You should try to absorb energy from any place where you can see abundance.

## 3. Breathing money

This technique is connected to the one explained in the previous point. You should sit down in a quiet place and imagine that you are breathing gold powder. From the metaphysical perspective, gold is the colour of prosperity. You must imagine inhaling this pure gold powder. See this powder pervading every cell of your body.

Another way to use this tool is to imagine thousands of pound notes entering your nose and filling your body. As you envision this, try to feel more prosperous. You should imagine that this money is floating and you have easy access to it. Feel that you can breathe this money in as easily and effortlessly as if it were air.

## 4. Creating a void

There is a principle that states that any void always tends to be filled with energy. Everything in the universe is pervaded by energy of difference frequencies. According to this perspective, each time you create a "void", the universe tends to fill it as soon as possible.

From this perspective, for example, you can open a bank account destined to be used for money you expect to receive. You don't have to deposit any money in that account. However, by keeping that bank account open, it will act like a natural attractor for your future incomes. The account will not be empty for long. This empty account will tend to attract the money to be deposited in it.

You can also buy blank notepads and include titles in their covers such as "new funds", "new properties", "new businesses" or "new clients". Leave them blank. The void generated by the notepads will attract those objects or people to your life.

## 5. Shower technique

It is important to highlight that when you take a shower, you clean your physical body, but you also cleanse your energetic field called your aura. The aura is an energetic field that pervades your body and connects your being with your environment.

Each time you take a shower you should imagine the cleansing of the energetic body. You must visualise all negative energy in your body being washed away. Then see yourself being showered with loving radiant energy. It is important to do this exercise when you are under the shower because the water falling on you will make this wrapping energy more real to your senses. It is advisable to practise this exercise early in the morning after you wake up. You can also do this just before going to bed.

A variation of this technique is suggested by Roberts. This author suggests that you should image being showered by pennies or notes. A tremendous amount of money is falling on you, like heavy rain. You can make this image more vivid, seeing high piles of money surrounding your body.

## 6. White loving light

This is a very well-known exercise commonly used in Metaphysics. You visualise a beam of white loving light entering the top of your head. This ray of light comes from the unlimited universal field. This ray is originated in the boundless universal provision. The beam fills each part of your body as it goes downwards.

Feel the ray going through your feet and out of them towards the centre of the planet. Once it reaches the centre of Earth, see the ray ascending and entering the soles of your feet again going upwards throughout your body. Feel how this energy nurtures your body with the unlimited resources of planet Earth.

This Earth light continues going upwards filling your whole body. The beam coming from the Earth meets, at your heart area, with the energy coming from the Universe. Both energies, from Earth and Universe, get fused in a radiant ball of energy.

You should imagine that, through your heart, you breathe that loving light in and out. This light continues pervading all your cells; feel that radiant beam of light surrounding your body.

Then imagine extending that light to your house, neighbourhood and city. After this imagine that loving light impregnating your country, the planet and the whole cosmos.

The ray of light that you use in this technique is a radiant pure white light. However you can also use a golden beam of light. As it was said before, from the metaphysical perspective, gold is the colour related to abundance.

## 7. Violet ray of light

This is a very ancient metaphysical technique. You should imagine being wrapped up by a violet beam of light. From the metaphysical viewpoint violet is the colour of transmutation.

Imagine that you are totally pervaded by that violet beam that comes from above. You should imagine that the ray of light is filling your body completely. Feel this beam of light cleansing each part of your body and transmuting your energy instantly. You can visualise this beam of light, as if it was a violet flame that burns all impurities and imperfections.

Apply this violet ray to places where you feel there is negative energy. See all the nooks of that place being pervaded by the flame which consumes all negative vibrations within it.

When you apply this technique, you can state the following invocation *"Dear Saint Germain please let this violet ray transmute any negative causes and effects in my life and convert them into love, prosperity and health"* Saint Germain is an enlightened spiritual master that is in charge of the violet ray. After finishing with this exercise, you can express your gratitude to the Universe.

## 8. Pyramid protection

The exercises explained in the previous points can be complemented with this technique. This protective tool is called pyramid shield. You must imagine that your body is surrounded by the four sides of a pyramid totally made of crystal. The sides of the pyramid must encircle you so that you end up inside the pyramid in its central part. You should begin first by being covered by the front side, then the back side, thirdly the left side and finally the right side.

You can use as many pyramids as you want to protect your energy. It is said that one pyramid gives you total protection for your energetic body for one hour. So if you want to be protected all day, you would have to use between 14 to 16 pyramids

## 9. Magnet technique

This technique is generally well-known by people familiar with metaphysical topics. Despite its simplicity, this tool happens to be very effective. This method can be used in several ways.

The first way to apply this tool is to get rid of any negative energy. This is based on the premise that every day we generally unwittingly absorb all types of energy from people, objects and our environment in general. This energy can be either positive or negative.

In order to apply this technique, you should imagine four big magnets around your body, one on every side of your body, another in front of you and the last one behind you. Visualise these magnets attracting all the negative energy that is pervading your body. You may visualise objects representing that energy getting stuck on the magnets. Visualise that this detrimental energy is effortlessly expelled from your body. The negative energy becomes glued to the magnets.

You can also place additional magnets above your head and below your feet for the same purpose. Use small magnets for areas of your body that you feel are more charged with negative energy. After this, imagine that you push the magnets far away. See those magnets, now loaded with negative energy from your body, disappear from your sight.

You can repeat this exercise the amount of times that you consider necessary. It is advisable to do this exercise at least once a day, if possible very late at night. If you do this properly, you will feel your body become lighter and the energy flowing in a much more lively fashion. You will feel your vibration heighten, which will accelerate the materialisation of your desires.

There is a second way to use magnets. Visualie that you have a big magnet inside you, a very powerful one. You should imagine that this magnet attracts large amounts of money towards you. This money can also attract any other desired object, such as a house, a car, one million pounds etc.

### 10. Paint brush technique

This is also a very well known technique in some metaphysical circles. In order to use this tool, first of all, assess the current state of your body energy. Try to see how the energy in your body is at present. Ask yourself questions such as *"What are the colours, shape and consistency of this energy?"* and *"Are there any shadows or obscure spots in my body energy?"* Try to visualise and sense the qualities of the energy in your body in detail.

Then visualise how the energy was, in a specific time in the past when you felt prosperous. For example, you can recall a moment when you collected a certain amount of money, or a time when you carried out a business activity successfully. You can also select moments in which you felt happy, exhilarated or any other energy state that you want to evoke. See those qualities in your body; observe the details of their colour, shape and consistency.

Instead of only using one past experience, you can use many memories of different times when you felt the same type of energy, for example, abundance. This will help you assess the qualities of that specific type of energy in more detail. For example, in the case of prosperity  recollect many different times in the past that you felt exhilarated because of having received money. Ask yourself *"What are the man characteristics of this energy?"*

Then compare your current state of energy with the one related to the past experience (in this example, the time when you felt prosperous). After this, imagine using a paint brush. See yourself dipping that brush in the field of energy of the past memory. With this energy on the brush, imagine giving several licks of paint all over your body. You must feel your whole body being covered with energy of the selected memory (in the example, prosperity). You will notice the shift in your energy and a raise in your overall vibration, which will help you with the manifestation of your desires.

Instead of using a brush you can imagine using a magic wand. With it, sprinkle the energy from your chosen memory all over your body.

## 11. Imagining your connection to the Universe

You can imagine yourself connected to a stream of brilliant light coming from the Universe. This light provides you with all the desires you have in mind. You should feel your intense connection with the Universe throughout this beam. You should also sense that the supportive universal flow is on the way to materialising all your dreams.

Feel the sensation that the universal forces are completely at your disposal. Know that they will simply obey your commands, as a faithful servant. Realise that the Universe is omnipotent, omniscient and almighty and it is always willing to fulfil your desires.

This tool can be applied to business activities. In these cases, consider yourself in close partnership with the all-supporting Universe. In that effect, this technique can be used every time you are carrying out any new business venture, such as asking for a bank loan, investing money, or designing a business plan, etc. In these cases bear in mind that the most important partner in these activities is the Universe.

Feel as if the Universe is supporting you in these activities, as a loyal partner. From this perspective, feel that the universal flow is to provide you with all the money, people, time and any other resource that you need to fulfil your goals.

# Chapter 18

# Other Techniques

*Money is the symbol of God's opinion, beauty, refinement, and abundance, and it should be used wisely, judiciously, and constructively to bless humanity in countless ways. When money is circulating freely in your life, you are economically healthy. When people began to hoard money, to put it away in tin boxes, and become charged with fear, there is economic illness.*
*Joseph Murphy*

## 1. Money as a friend

### 1.1. General aspects

At the beginning, you may think that this technique is a bit strange. However many metaphysical masters recognised this tool as one of the most powerful techniques to attract prosperity. Please think about this: *how can you attract more funds, if you treat money in a nasty manner or as undesired company?*

You must realise that you are actually pushing away your chances to be prosperous when you use statements like "*Money is the root of all evil*", "*Money is not for me*", "*Money is scarce*", or "*It's hard to get money*". At the beginning of this book you saw a list of other common negative connotations regarding money.

Even in the cases when you complain about your financial difficulties you are talking about money in a negative manner. In all these cases you are not considering money like a friend of yours. Each time that you talk or think negatively about money you don't perceive money as an amicable partner in your life. This radiates very low vibrations, which in turn pushes money away from you.

## 1.2. Application of the tool

So this technique is very simple and straightforward. Try to visualise money as if it was a very important friend of yours. In order to do so, try not to visualise this abstractly. If possible, try to envision money as a supportive friend, a person that you can talk to and confide in. If it is difficult to visualise a person representing money as a friend, you can apply this technique with real money, such as coins or notes.

See yourself getting on well with this supportive friend at all times. Imagine that you can engage in friendly conversations with this person, who represents money. You should also visualise yourself building a prosperous relationship with this money-partner. You can even imagine saying to this friend *"I like you"*, *"Thank you for staying with me"*, *"I will always appreciate you and care for you"* or *"Thank you for being so generous"*.

You must also imagine what money would need from you, as a close friend of yours. For example, you can ask yourself *"Does my friend want me to act in a certain way?"* If you have some doubts about how to act, imagine asking money about its needs, as your friend. Try to be attentive to receive its answer. You may receive significant intuitive insights about this.

You can daringly imagine giving this friend, which is money, some compliments, such as *"You are beautiful"*, or *"You are so attractive"*. All that praise must be heartfelt. Feel a loving bond that unites you with this friend; try to visualise this warm loving state in the area of your heart.

From this perspective, if you want to treat money as a supportive friend, you cannot be pushy, unaffectionate or careless with it. You should not be clinging onto money, or look desperate or needy. On the contrary, you should be grateful and respectful with money, as a friend of yours. Imagine telling money that you appreciate having its company in your life. You will see that when you are appreciative with money as a friend, it will accompany and support you much more over time.

## 1.3. Other applications of this technique

After practising these visualisations explained in the previous point, also apply the same principles about friendship to physical money. For example, you should begin to treat all money you come in contact with, for example, notes, coins and cheques with respect and affection.

This means that you treat real money in the same way as you would a close friend that you care for. Try to have a loving attitude to physical money each time you receive or give it. You should be thankful each time you come in contact with real money. Whenever possible you should show signals of loving care towards actual money, for example, by delivering compliments. This is a way of showing that you value money.

Besides, if you consider money as a friend, you should not behave with it in a punitive way. To put it simply, you should never ever criticise or deprecate money; remember that money is your dear friend, so you should only treat money respectfully and lovingly. If you criticise or moan about money you are actually repelling its company in your life.

Try to write down a description of your relationship with money. You can put this in pictures or sentences. *"How is your relationship with money now?"* and *"How do you want this to be? "*, *"What are the actions that you can take to have a better relationship with money?"* Some qualities you can consider for an ideal friendship relationship with money are: supportiveness, care, love, fun, etc. You can also make note of the most positive feelings you want to experience when being in contact with money. Then try to imagine experiencing those emotional states each time that you receive or give money.

## 1.4. Talking to money

You should imagine yourself talking to money openly. It is advisable to ask money questions about different topics, which you want to know more about. For example, some topics for questions you can ask are:

*Different ways of having a more significant and prosperous relationship with it*
*Negative patterns you tend to show when you relate to it*
*Tips to attract more affluence*
*Other lessons or advice money wants to give you to improve your life*

Visualise asking these questions to your friend, money, and then wait for its answers. In some cases, you can visualise yourself asking these questions, as well as writing them down on a piece of paper with your dominant hand. Then, wait for the answer, and try to write the first thing that comes to your mind with your non-dominant hand. Some say that writing with the non-dominant hand connects you to your inner wisdom.

You must ask these questions in a state of relaxation. If you are calm and relaxed, you are more likely to obtain prized insights. You can also apply this technique just after practising meditation.

### 1.5. Your attitude toward wealthy people

From this perspective, if you consider money as your friend, you should always be kind and respectful to people who have a lot of money, for example, millionaires or tycoons. Many people tend to criticise wealthy people using sentences like *"Filthy rich"* or other phrases. When you disapprove of rich people, you are radiating low vibrations, which push the manifestation of your dreams, of having more money, away.

For this reason, instead, you must have an appreciative and affectionate attitude to all people, even the wealthy. Think that they can also be friends of your friend, which is money. Don't feel jealous or envious because wealthy people also have a relationship with your friend, which is money. Be aware that your friendship with money is not exclusive. In fact your close friend, money, has a lot of other close friends. Feel OK with it. So you must treat your friend's friends with respect. Don't cast criticism or show any hatred towards them.

## 2. Cosmic Ordering

### 2.1. Main aspects

A writer called Mohr suggests a strategy called cosmic ordering. This strategy happens to be very simple but, at the same time, very effective. When you desire something in your life, such as more money or anything else, you must place a written order to the Universe. From this perspective you consider the Universe as a shop and you are requesting an item from it.

Your order to the Universe must include the specific things that you want, for example, a certain amount of money, a house, or any other stuff that you like. You must write down your order to the Universe. In that sense, this letter must be addressed to the universal force, using statements such *as "Dear Universe, "Dear Cosmos", "Dear God"* or any other of your preference.

In the first part of the letter, include a list of the items (products, experiences, etc.) that you want to order. List them below a heading that says "I want to order:" In a second part of this order you must include the feelings that you want to experience as part of the things that you are ordering.

In the third part of the letter, you must also include a brief list of your activities and thoughts in the meanwhile. That means how you will act and think during the period of time before the order from the Universe is delivered. Try to choose only thoughts and activities that radiate high vibrations. For example, you can state that you will meditate, visualise and have positive thoughts on a daily basis. You can also include any other of the tools seen in this book.

In the last part don't forget to sign the letter including your complete name (first name and surname). You must also include the words *"Thank you, thank you, thank you"*.

## 2.2. Other aspects of this technique

Once you write the order you must recite it aloud only once. If you want, you can spell out the content through an open window. After this, keep the order in a secretive place. Alternatively you can throw the letter into the toilet and flush it away. The whole of this procedure should be done in a good and relaxed mood. You should not comment about your order to anybody.

You can start writing orders to the Universe with little desires. When you see the first results, you can continue with bigger wishes. In your orders, you can also include the date by which your desires should be delivered. In that sense, you can include sentences like *"To be delivered by..."* When you write the orders, always use clear and positive sentences. Include only what you want, instead of what you don't desire.

After placing the order, you should forget it, if possible. Be detached from the result of that order, keep carrying on with your daily activities, without even thinking about the order you placed. This attitude of detachment will accelerate the delivery of your order.

In this book it was explained that when you are attached to the outcomes, you are blocking the manifestation of this desire. The same principle applies to the delivery of your order from the Universe. For this reason, let go of any expectations about the order and its delivery.

When your order was delivered you should acknowledge receipt of it. In order to do so, you must express your gratitude to the universe because your order was delivered. You can also celebrate the delivery. You can use the techniques explained in the chapter about *"Gratitude"* in this book.

## 3. The Golden Key

### 3.1. Main aspects of this technique

This is a very effective method to attract more money, or to solve any problem in your life. The golden key was originally proposed by Emmet Fox. This simple technique is also called scientific prayer. It's a tool that you can apply straightforwardly. However don't get tricked by its simplicity.

This method is, in fact, excessively simple, but also very powerful. Every time that you have a problem, such as financial difficulties, you don't have to dwell on them. Instead, you must only focus on God. Think about God's characteristics such as life, love, harmony, unity, peacefulness, omnipresence, truth, wholeness, wisdom, joy and almightiness. Think about all the positive traits of God's presence; don't think about anything else, even your problem.

In that sense, Butterworth says that *"God is the allness of ever-present substance in which we live, move and have being... The whole of God is present at every point in space at the same time"*. From this perspective you must realise that you are always entitled to be prosperous effortlessly. Everything that you have or that you will have, even money, comes from God. You must consider God as your celestial warehouse, which provides you with everything in your life.

With the application of the Golden Key, that is thinking about God instead of the problem, you dispel any negative conditions, even those that appear completely unsolvable at present. When you are thinking about God and his traits, you are vibrating at a very high level, which accelerates the manifestation of all your desires.

Nevertheless, when you use this tool, you should not be focusing on the problem. Your undivided attention must be placed on God's qualities. You must only concentrate on God's characteristics, and nothing else.

To put this simply, you don't have to think of anything else, but God. This simple tool is very effective because it helps you cast any negative emotional state, such as doubt or fear, aside. The application of this technique removes any blockage or limitation regarding the materialisation of your dreams.

When you use this technique, by thinking about God, you are actually getting in contact with God. With the use of this tool you are recognising God as the most powerful force. You faithfully believe that God acts directly, with no intermediaries, to solve all your problems. You know that God will provide you with everything that you wish. In fact, you also realise that you are a conduit through which God acts with his almighty power.

### 3.2. Other ways of using this technique

There is another way to use this tool. In that effect, you can say *"I am about to apply the Golden Key to... (name the difficulty)"*. Then you turn your mind away from the problem, and only focus on God's traits. In this way you are letting God lead the whole process of manifestation of good conditions. With the application of this tool, you become the channel through which the divine intervention of God operates.

There is a very important caveat on the application of this tool. In order for this technique to be successful, you should always be faithful and receptive. When you have this attitude, you will certainly see your problems solved spontaneously. Emmet Fox also suggests using sayings such as *"God is with me"* or *"The only power is God's"*.

From this perspective, you must become accustomed to seeing everything in your life from the perspective of God's provision. See your own environment and your financial activities from an abundance perspective. In that sense, according to some masters, when you have financial problems, you should say *"The truth of this situation is (name any of God's attributes)"*.

You should try to see the truth underneath any troublesome situation. Realise that problems are only appearances. The only truth that exists beneath any apparent difficulty is the presence of God's divine attributes. It was explained that those traits are love, beauty, harmony, wisdom, bliss, among others. Always dwell on them, turn your mind away from the apparent difficulties, if you want your problems to solve naturally.

When you reject the appearances of a problem, and focus only on the truth underneath it, the difficulty tends to be automatically solved. By focusing on God's characteristics and dwelling on them, those traits become present in your life, and as a consequence, your problem dissipates effortlessly.

# Appendices

## Some Other Tips about Abundance

### Appendix A
### Silence

This tool is simple but also very effective. You should devote some minutes each day to total silence. This means not talking to anybody, even you. In order to do so, your mind must be pervaded by total stillness and muteness. Try to make the habit of staying in silence. Consider your mental quietness as your peaceful inner shelter. This state allows the ceaseless murmuring of your mind to rest for a while. It also refuges you from negative external influences.

Silence is a refreshing state for your mind, in which you can tap into your inner resources. When you are silent, your mind reposes from its continual over-analytical working. As a consequence, you become in contact with your inner wisdom. Your mind is temporarily switched off, regarding its constant labelling of circumstances. For this reason, your mental energy tends to be higher after a moment of silence.

The objective of this practice is to create a blank in your mind, as long as possible. In order to stay in silence, many authors like Tolle recommend that, each time a thought comes to your mind, you should observe it as an external witness, and let it go. You can visualise the thought as if it were a passing cloud in the sky. You should never judge the thoughts that are coming up, just let them go past. Then try to shift your attention again to the still state.

In order to experience stillness, focus on your respiration. This will make it easier for you to maintain the silent state. Another helpful way to achieve this state is to focus on your third eye (on the area of the sixth chakra). You can also concentrate on the area of the top of your head (seventh chakra).

When you do this exercise, at the beginning, your thoughts may become turbulent. This is a natural defence mechanism of your mind, which is not accustomed to absolute silence. However if you can stay focused on achieving the silent state, the chattering voice of your mind will subside.

You can obtain this silent state through meditation. However you can also try to enter this state when you carry out your daily activities. In this second case, you don't need to have a specific time or a place to be still, as compared with the meditation practice.

Your silent mind allows your connection with the universal forces. This state of muteness is ideal to use affirmations or visualisation techniques. A state of silence makes these tools more effective. In that state, your limiting beliefs cannot hinder the manifestation of your desires. When you are in silence you are also more receptive to intuitive insights.

Tolle gives some tips to achieving a state of silence. In order to achieve this state you should focus on the next thought about to come. That means you should purposefully wait for the thought that is about to sneak into your mind. You can also pay attention to the silence pervading your environment. Another way is to focus on the energy of your body, without any judgement. You should feel the energy pervading your body. All these techniques help you to connect to the present moment.

## Appendix B
## Flow

The state of flow has been studied by many psychologists. From the metaphysic perspective, being in a state of flow is a good way to attract abundance. When you are in the flow you are fully present. If you are carrying out a specific activity, you are to be fully engrossed in it. When you are in the flow, you enjoy the activity itself; you don't consider it as a means to a goal. When you are flowing you are not focused on the past or future. Instead, your mind is fixated on the present moment.

In the flow state you are totally abandoned to your current experience; you are totally lost in the process. In that sense, you do not look for any kind of control over things. In this state, your vision becomes clearer and your focus more accurate. Your concentration resembles a laser ray; you only focus on the essential and ignore the rest. You also experience a state of harmony and intense glee. In this state, time and space seem to disappear. Besides, you tend to be very prolific; ideas come to your mind hastily and effortlessly. You feel as if you were channelling your creation.

It is important to pinpoint that the activities that get you in a state of flow vary from person to person significantly. For this reason, it's important to assess all your activities and ask yourself *"Which of those activities gives timeless joy?"*

Some examples of these activities that can produce the flow state are: listening to pleasant music, reading a good book, walking in a park, watching a film, dancing, having sex, among others. You will easily discover your favourite ones, which might be different from the ones mentioned. It is only a matter of paying attention to your feelings when you perform these activities. You will discover that when an activity puts you in a state of flow, you lose the notion of time and space. Inspired actions are generally performed in a state of flow. This type of activity was explained in the chapter related to objectives.

When you perform activities in a state of flow, you cast away any impediment and fear. You also release tension and anxiety. In that sense, you radiate very high vibrations, which will help you manifest your desires much more easily. The flow state always raises your energy; you are more connected to the universal forces.

# Appendix C
# Co-operation

*Collaboration and reciprocity are natural and yet in the world we inhabit, competition and the fear of scarcity often block us from being with one another... Collaboration becomes the circuitry through which the energy, attention and resources of sufficiency flow and are continually renewed.*
*Lynne Twist*

From the metaphysical perspective, all resources in the Universe are inexhaustible. In that effect, if you want to attract more prosperity in your life, you don't have to compete with others. Each time you consider others as potential or actual competitors, you are focusing on scarcity. From the scarcity viewpoint, you believe that you can only get more resources, including money, if others have less. By focusing on scarcity, you use a win-lose approach, because you believe that the only way for you to win is at the expense of others.

There are many sociological studies that state that people learnt how to compete with others over time. In this sense, competing is not an innate human quality; it is not inherent to human essence. Instead competing is a skill that you learnt during your life. You see how other people compete with others and you tend to replicate their behaviour, in most of the cases unwittingly.

It's important to pinpoint that a competitive approach, from the viewpoint of Metaphysics is based on intense feelings of fear. In that sense, Wattles, states that *"You are to become a creator, not a competitor; you are going to get what you want, but in such a way that when you get it every other man will have more than he has now... Riches secured on the competitive plane are never satisfactory and permanent"* When you compete you tend to focus on others, instead of concentrating on yourself. Moreover competing with others is a waste of your vital energy. By competing, you tend to use your precious energy to defeat others, which you consider as "enemies" or "rivals". When you compete you radiate negative energy because you are acting based on fear.

When you compete you primarily focus on others and compare them to you to outpace them. By competing, you cannot concentrate only on yourself to improve your own value and performance, according to your own parameters; when you compete, your focus is always outside, on others. Competition only generates negative energy that pushes away the materialisation of your desires.

Instead, when you cooperate with others you radiate high vibrations. Co-operation is based on love and affection to others; you are not fearful of them. Co-operation is based on trust, you confide in others, so you can carry out joint activities with them. By co-operating with others, you are generating high quality energy, based on lovingness and support. This type of vibration accelerates the manifestation of your dreams.

It is important to highlight that not all cultural environments deal with competition and co-operation in the same way. In that sense, there are some cultures that are more oriented to co-operation than to competition. Instead other cultural contexts prefer competitive environments.

One of the most effective ways to attract more abundance in all areas of your life is to focus on co-operation whenever possible. You should ask yourself questions like: *"What people am I willing to help to get more money?", "What people are willing to help me get more money?", "How can I generate more money with these partners?"*

Co-operative relationships are always expansive; they are based on a win-win approach. All parties benefit from the relationship. They are based on a prosperity mentality, as compared to the competitive perspective.

When you co-operate you recognise your unique resources

(skills, personality, etc.) and you know that can be shared with others. You also believe that others' resources can assist you. In fact, from a co-operation perspective, you can make a significant and diverse contribution to others and vice versa, which improves the situation of all involved. By co-operating you are recognising your interconnection with others, and honouring it.

For this reason, you should approach people from a co-operative perspective whenever possible. You will realise that most of the time you can share information, material resources, and intangibles (feelings, support, etc.) with them.

You can argue that you cannot co-operate with people that have similar objectives or the same activities as yours. This tenet is based on a scarcity mindset. It implicitly states that, in life, you have to vie for scanty resources with others. However always bear in mind that, in order to succeed, you don't have to outpace others.

Always focus on enhancing your unique value, and let others develop theirs. If possible try to co-operate with them to progress together. Your main purpose in life must be to improve yourself continually, without trying to defeat others. Focus on your positive skills, your talents. If possible, share them with others, in a co-operative manner. Do not try to beat others, but try to improve yourself over time.

When you relate to others, from the co-operative perspective, you have an abundance mentality. When you have a prosperity mindset, you can relate to others bringing about benefits for all involved. You can share your resources and skills with others and vice versa. You can get more fulfilled and fearless.

You can also have a co-operative attitude when you own a business. In that case, you should think about the ways to co-operate with others. In that effect, you can develop co-operative alliances with intermediaries, suppliers and other companies (the ones that have complementary products to yours and also rival businesses). The co-operative agreements could cover different areas, such as: joint promotion, joint transportation, joint research and development, joint manufacturing, among others. Some benefits of co-operating with other organisations are: reductions of costs, complementation of resources (such as: technology, experience, contacts, technical information, funds, etc.), increase in negotiation power with outsiders, betterment of quality and diversity of the products or services of the joint project, among others. In general, co-operative agreements with other companies tend to produce synergetic results.

As a business owner, you can also co-operate with your community, for example, through the sponsorship of social events, throug foundations, donations, etc. You can co-operate with your customers, by providing them with complete and credible information about products, providing them with incentives (discounts, free samples, gifts, promotions, and other incentives), assisting them before, during and after sales, among other activities. When you use a co-operative approach with customers, you are offering them higher value, which makes them more loyal to your business. You don't even have to worry about potential competitors because customers are likely to choose your company naturally.

You can also co-operate with the environment, by carrying out activities that are environmentally friendly, such as use of green technology, recycling, etc. In all cases, the co-operative activities mentioned above tend to benefit your company financially and also improve your image and reputation.

## Appendix D
## Think about new ways to make money

*How can you expect to become rich if you haven't decided what rich means toyou?*
*Tom Hopkins*

Another point to analyse is creative ways to make money. In that effect, you should be devoting, at least, thirty minutes a day to write down new ideas about that. Try to list as many alternatives as possible. Think about options that can be implemented, either with effort and effortlessly.

You should never limit your thinking to traditional activities. Try to develop a wide range of options. You may include, for example, options such as selling goods on the Internet, offering seminars, buying stocks, importing or exporting, renting properties, etc. Take note of any new ideas that come to your mind. Review your notes frequently.

The list of ideas should be as overarching as possible. You do not have to refrain yourself from including any idea, even if, at first, it appears to be a ridiculous one. In that sense, you should be as prolific as possible. In a second phase, you will have time to weed out the ideas that sound less practical or feasible.

After you have written down the list, rate them according to how comfortable you feel with them. In order to do this, try to consider if the options are congruent with your purpose and skills. Then ask yourself *"Does this alternative allow me to add value to people and solve their problems?"*, *"Does this option make me feel passionate?"* and *"Does this affect my integrity in a positive way?"* Select the ways to obtain money that have an affirmative answer to those three questions. Other important criteria that you can take into account to select the best alternatives are: availability of resources, costs involved, information in hand, complexity of activity, potential training needed, contingencies, estimated profitability, among others.

Some other questions that you can ask yourself to select the most appropriate alternatives are:

*How can I provide value in a unique way to many people?*
*How can I be financially independent and at the same time empowered and happy?*

*How can I increase my income in a socially responsible and ethical way?*
*How are other people executing that activity in a similar way?*
*How can I do that differently?*
*How can I satisfy people's needs and be more prosperous?*
*Can my options expand indefinitely?*
*Can I make money in partnership with others?*
*How can I be more prosperous effortlessly?*
*How can I add value to a wide audience?*

You can use creative techniques to generate new ideas about earning money. All these techniques will help you think in an unconventional and more flexible fashion. Some well-known tools that can be used are:

*Brainstorming:* This is a collective, synergic and unrestrained exposition of ideas. People gather in a group and expose their ideas freely.
*Search of analogies:* Analogies are similarities present in other fields, for example, you can see what procedures of other sectors can be applied to your business.
*Random combination*: This is the combination of topics that are apparently unconnected, for example, money and luck.
*Reframing problems*: Reformulating the problem regarding money, making it more general, more specific, with focus on long term and short term, highlighting primary factors and secondary ones, looking for qualitative advantages and quantitative ones.
*Posing hypothetical questions:* Asking questions based on assumptions such as *"what if...?"*
*Mindmapping:* Drawing graphs with the main idea to analyse in the central place, and showing the ramifications to secondary ideas that come from the main one.

All these creative techniques are focused on challenging traditional perspectives, assumptions or any other limitations about money. You must be open but also discerning. Keep track of all the ideas you are gathering up.

You must also think of ideas to generate income, without working. These activities are commonly known as passive income generators. Some examples of passive income are royalties from books, selling on the Internet with an automatic platform, renting properties, interest in a bank account, dividends from shares, etc.

Other questions that you can ask yourself are:

*What are the shortcomings and advantages of each alternative?*
*What is the technical knowledge necessary for each alternative?*
*Which is the option that represents the best high reward – low effort ratio?*

You can model wealthy people. Take them as an example to emulate for your activities regarding money. There are different ways to know more about prosperous people's mindsets, for example you can read books or interviews about them. You can also pay attention to any criticism cast on them by other people, which will give you useful insights too. Some questions that you can ask yourself when analysing these prosperous role models:

*What are the main qualities of their mindsets?*
*How do they act differently from others?*
*How can I model their behaviour and their way of thinking?*

You can emulate their behaviour and mindset. In order to do so, try to model their beliefs, their way of thinking. Also pay attention to their posture, body language how they move. However, you should never worship wealthy people. Instead, feel that you are also capable of being prosperous too. You should only take these people as models or guidance for your activities. In that sense, you must find your authentic way to do things, which makes you feel comfortable and gives you money doing less.

By knowing more about other people making money, you may experience a sense of relief. You may realise that these people are not the only ones deserving of making money; you can have abundance in your life too. In that effect, you must realise that you can always go beyond your current circumstances, because you are limitless in your essence. Another question that you can ask yourself is: *If these wealthy people were in my current financial situation; how would they improve it?* You are likely to get interesting insights from this question.

Also you should think about how you can use other people's resources, instead of using your own. This concept is called leverage and it can help you earn money doing less. Eker gives some examples of leverage: using other people's capabilities, using media to promote your products, using agents or sellers to commercialise your goods, selling products before they are launched, using others' money (banks, financial institutions, etc.), getting sponsorship for your activities, among others.

You can also get in contact with different groups to resort to new ideas. In that sense, network meetings and mastermind groups are very useful for this purpose.

## Appendix E
## Money education

*Ignorance is easier, but it is often the result of fear.*
*Donald Trump*

Education improves your intellectual skills and opens up new perspectives. This present book is an example of educative activities. In that sense, the knowledge exposed in this book helps you do things differently regarding money.

By getting applicable knowledge about money topics, you will raise your level of awareness about your financial position. This will make you feel more secure regarding money issues. In that effect, new knowledge is a resource that can help you attract more prosperity.

According to McKenna, the knowledge that you have about money can be obtained in two ways: a) codified sources such as seminars, videos and books, which is also called explicit knowledge b) through experience and insights, which is called implicit knowledge. Whenever possible, you should get both implicit and explicit knowledge.

Education should always be considered as an investment not an expense. Knowledge allows you to be freer. In fact, knowledge about money topics can help you reduce your dependence on others.

You should be incorporating learnable skills about different money topics, such as finance, investment and other business subjects. This will help you plan your activities much more effectively. You also feel less ignorant and hesitative when you have to take action related to your financial position. You are likely to feel more in control of your financial activities, and in general, more in charge of your life. Useful knowledge is like switching on a bulb in a dark room; in that sense, knowledge gives you more clarity on things, you don't get deceived by appearances.

Education also enhances your discernment and makes your thoughts more lucid. You will feel more self-assured and collected. When you are more knowledgeable about money issues, you are likely to approach problems with much more ease. You will also have more dominion over difficult financial times.

With appropriate knowledge about money in hand, it will also be easier for you to discover hidden opportunities in every situation. New knowledge will help develop your mental processes and have a more lucid rationale. Education will help you think in different ways about money, widening your perspectives on it.

The focus on your own education should be continuous and proactive. You can always learn something new about prosperity, and in general, money issues. From this viewpoint, the knowledge you can obtain is limitless. In fact, you can be training yourself until the end of your days. For this reason, try to take the initiative to get trained. Each time you get useful knowledge, you are actually adding value to yourself, and this will certainly pay off later.

As was said before, there are different ways to get more knowledge, books, seminars, courses, videos, etc. In relation to money education, try to focus on knowledge that provides you with new skills. So do not concentrate so much on the certificate that you can get.

Instead, focus on the abilities and new perspectives you can incorporate. Try to give priority to sources of knowledge that can make you gain experience about money skills. This may be working for a company or analysing practical cases. Also look for knowledge about money that can be applied in your life straightforwardly.

# Bibliography


Allen James. (No date) *As a Man Thinketh.* G.P.Putman's Sons New York

Allen James (1906) *From Poverty to Power.* The Science Press Republic Building Chicago

Allen James (1996) *The Path of Prosperity.* Kessinger Publisher. USA

Allen James (2005) *The Eight Pillars of Prosperity.* Kessinger Publisher. USA

Anthony Robert (2007) *Beyond Positive Thinking A No-Nonsense Formula for Getting The Results You Want.* Morgan James. New York

Anthony Robert (2012) *How to Make your Mind a Money Magnet. The Secret of Never Ending Cash-Flow.* www.thesecretofdeliberatecreation.com

Arewa Caroline Shola. (2010) *Energy 4 Life. High Energy, Conscious Living.* O-Books UK

Atkinson William Walker (1908) *Mind-Power. The Secret of Mental Magic.* The Progress Company. London

Babson Roger W (1920) *Fundamentals of Prosperity.* Fleming Revel Company. London

Bach David (2004) *The Automatic Millionaire.* Broadway Books. USA

Bailes Frederick (2004) *Basic Principles of the Science of Mind.* De Vors Publications California

Baron Robert A. and Michael J. Kaisher. (2001) *Essentials of Psychology.* Allyn and Bacon. USA

Byrne Rhonda. (2010) *The Power.* Simon and Schuster UK

Butler-Bowdon Tom (2008) *50 Prosperity Classics.* Nicholas Brealey Publishing London

Butterworth Eric (2011) *Spiritual Economics. The Principles and Process of True Prosperity.* Unity Canada

Carlyle Marie Claire. (2010) *How to Become a Money Magnet.* Hay House. UK

Carlyle-Marie Claire (2012) *Money Magnet Mindset. Tools to Keep You and Your Money on Track.* Hay House. UK

Childre Doc, Howard Martin and Donna Beech. (2000) *The Heartmath Solution.* Harper Collins USA

Chilton David (2008) *The Wealthy Barber.* Prima Publishing. USA

Chopra Deepak (1997) *Las Siete Leyes Espirituales del Exito.* Norma Argentina

Chopra Deepak (1998) *Creating Affluence. The a-to-z steps to a richer life.* Amber Allen Publishing San Rafael

Cialidini Robert (2009) *Influence. Science and Practice.* Pearson Education USA

Clason George S. (1009) *The Richest Man In Babylon.* Signet USA

Copeland Kenneth (1974) *The Laws of Prosperity.* Kenneth Copeland Publications. Texas

Davis Martha, Robbins Eshelman Elizabeth and McKay Matthew (2008) *The Relaxation and Stress Reduction Book.* New Harbinger Publications Inc. USA

Denning and Philips (2001) *Practical Guide to Creative Visualization. Manifest your Desires.* Llewellyn Publications. USA

Dominguez Joe and Vicki Robin (1999) *Your Money or Your life.* Penguin Books. USA

Dowskin Hale (2007) *The Sedona Method Course.* Sedona Training Associates. USA

Dowskin Hale and Lester Levinson (2001) *Happiness is Free and It's Easier than You Think.* Sedona Training Associates. USA.

Dyer Wayne (1978) *Tus zonas erróneas.* Grijalbo. Barcelona

Dyer Wayne W. (1992) *Tus zonas mágicas.* Grijalbo. Barcelona

Dyer Wayne (2004) *The Power of Intention.* Hay House Inc. USA

Dyer Wayne (1998) *Manifest your destiny. The Nine Spiritual Secrets for Getting Everything that You Want.* Harper Perennial. New York

Eker T. Harv (1996) *Speedwealth*. Peak Potential Publishing. Canada

Eker T. Harv (2009) *Secret of the Millionaire Mind*. Piatkus Great Britain

Emoto, Masaru (2004) *The Hidden Messages in Water*. Beyond Words Publishing. Hillsboro. Oregon

Fanning P (1994) *Visualization for Change*. New Harbinger Publications. Oakland

Fiddes Dax (2008) *The Alchemy of Abundance*. Mercury Publishing. Australia

Fillmore Charles (2005) *Prosperity*. Unity House. Unity Village MO

Fisher Mark (2010) *An Instant Millionaire. A Tale of Wisdom and Wealth*. New World Library. California

Fone Helena (2008) *Emotional Freedom Technique for Dummies*. John Wiley and Sons Ltd. England

Fox Emmet (2006) *The Mental Equivalent* Kessinger Publisher. USA

Fox Emmet (2011) *The Golden Key* Literary Licensing LLC USA

Gage Randy (2003) *Accept your Abundance*. Prime Concepts Group, Inc.

Gawain Shakti (2001) *Creative Visualization. Use the Power of Your Imagination to Create What You Want in Your life*. New World Library. Novato. California

Gendin E. (1981) *Focusing*. Bantan Books. New York

Given Charles. (1995) *More Wealth Without Risk*. Pocket Books. USA

Goi James Jr.(2007) *Hot to Attract Money Using Mind power*. Infinity USA

Goleman Daniel (1995) *Emotional Intelligence. Why It Can Matter More than IQ*. Bantam Books. USA

Grayson Stuart (1986) *The Ten Demmandments of Prosperity*. Dodd, Mead and Company. New York

Hallan Andew (2011) *Millionaire Teacher*. John Wiley and Sons.

Singapore
Haanel Charles (1916) *The Master Key System*. Psychology Publishing Saint Louis
Harris Herbert (2005) *The Twelve Universal Laws of Success*. The LifeSkill Institute Inc. Wilmington NC
Hawkins David R. (2002) *Power Vs Force. The Hidden Determinants of Human Behaviour*. Hay House USA
Hicks Esther and Jerry (2004) *Ask And It Is Given. Learning To Manifest Your Desires*. Hay House USA
Hicks Esther and Jerry (2008) *Money and the Law of Attraction*. Hay House Padstow Cornwall
Hill Napoleon (1960) *Think and Grow Rich*. Fawcett Crest. New York
Hilton Suzan (2002) *Feng Shui de la abundancia*. Urano. Barcelona
Hoplkins Tom (1984) *The Official Guide to Success*. Warner Books Inc. New York
Jeffers Susan (1991) *Feel the Fear and Do It Anyway*. Croydon
Kennerley Helen (2009) *Overcoming anxiety*. Constable and Robinson. London
Law Kwan (2004) *Feng Shui Edaf*. Espana
Levinson Lester (1993) *Keys to Ultimate Freedom. Thoughts and Talks on Personal Transformation*. Sedona Institute. USA
Marina Rebecca (No date) *30 Angel Steps to Prosperity*. Celebration Healing Publishing USA
Mc. Cullough C.J.M. and Woods Mann R. (1994) *La ansiedad*. Editorial Sudamericana. Buenos Aires
Mc. Raney David (2011) *You Are Not So Smart*. Dutton USA
Kusternacher Werner Tiki and Lothar J. Seiwert. *Como simplificar a sua vida*. (2006) Editorial Presenca Lisboa
LeCron Leslie (1974) *Autohipnotismo*. Editorial Diana Mexico
Losier Michael (2008) *Law of Attraction. The Secret Behind The Secret*. Hodder Mobius. UK
Matthews A. M. (1998) *Siete Claves para Vivir in Calma*. Vergara. Buenos Aires

McKenna Paul (2004) Change your Life in Seven Days. Transworld. UK

McKenna Paul (2008) I can make you rich. Bantan Press. UK

McKenna Eugene (2012) *Business Psychology and Organizational Behaviour.* Psychology Press. East Sussex

Mc Kenzie Eleanor (2009) *The Reiki Biible. The Definitive Guide to the Art of Reiki.* Bounty Books. China

Mendez, Conny (1991) *Metafisica 4 en 1.* Bienes Laconica C.A. Venezuela

Mendez, Conny (1994) *Metafisica 4 en 1.* Bienes Laconica C.A. Venezuela

Metafisica XII (1993) *CZ Ediciones*. Argentina

Metafisica X (1993) *CZ Ediciones*. Argentina

Mohr Barbel. (2011) *The Cosmic Ordering Service.* Hodder.& Stoughton. UK

Mohr Barbel (2011) *The 21 Golden Rules for Cosmic Ordering*. Hay House. UK

Morgan Stanley (2001) *Claves Sencillas para Ganar Dinero Planeta.* Buenos Aires

Mulford Prentice. (2009) *Thoughts are Things*. Seeds of Life Publishing. USA

Murphy Joseph. (1963) *The Power of your Subconscious Mind.* Prentice Hall Inc. USA.

Murphy Joseph (2010) *How to Attract Money*. Martino Publishing Mansfield Centre USA

Nemeth Maria. (1999) *The Energy of Money. A Spiritual Guide to Financial and Personal Fulfillment.* Ballantine Wellspring

Nichol Lee (edit.) (2003) *The Essential David Bohm*. Routledege London

Nightingale Earl. (2012) *The Strangest Secret of Succeeding in the World Today.* Nightingale Conant. USA

Olson Dale (1994) *Knowing Your Intuitive Mind*. Crystalline Publications Eugene OR

Ortner Nich and Others (2008) *15 Ways of Health, Happiness and*

*Abundance.* Tryitoneverything.com

Ortner Nich and Others. *Tapping your Way to Health, Happines and Abundance.* www.thetappingsolution.com

Osho (2004) Meditation. *The First and Last Freedom.* Saint Martin's Griffin. New York

Pauley Thomas l. And Penelope J. Pauley. (1999) *I'm Rich Beyond My Wildest Dreams I am I am I am.* Berkley Books New York

Price John Randolph (1996) *The Abundance Book.* Hay House. USA

Ponder Catherine (2011) *The Dynamic Laws of Prosperity.* Martino Fine Books. USA

Ponder Catherine (2010) *Open your Mind to Receive.* Princeton Licensing Group. USA

Price John R. (2005) *The Abundance Book.* Hay House Carlsbad CA

Proctor Bob. (2002) *The Science of Getting Rich.* Life Success Production

Rae Morgana. *Proven Steps to be a Money Magnet.* Internet Conference. September 2012

Ramsey Dave (2009) *The Total Money Makeover.* Thomas Nelson. Tennessee

Remele Patricia (1995) *Money Freedom. Finding Your Inner Source of Wealth.* A.R.E. Press. Virginia

Resnick Stella (1998) Re*encontrar el placer Urano.* Barcelona

Robert Stephanie (2004) *Fast Feng Shui for Prosperity.* Lotus Pond Press. Kahului.

Robinson Ken (2009) *The Element. How Finding Your Passion Changes Everything,* Pengin Books. England.

Robbins Anthony (1996) *How to Make the Impossible Possible.* Berkley Books New York.

Robbins Anthony (1997) *Mensaje a un amigo.* Grijalbo Mondadori Barcelona

Robinson Lynn A. (2004) *Real Prosperity. Using the Power of Intuition to Create Financial and Spiritual Abundance.* Andrews McMeel Publishing Kansas City MO

Roman Sanaya and Duane Packer. (1988) *Creating Money. Key to Abundance.* H.J. Kramer Inc. Tiburon California

Rossbach Sarah and Master Lin Yun (1996) *Master Lin Yun Living Colour. Guide to Feng Shui and the Art of Colour.* Kodansha International. USA

Rosenberg Bobby (2002) *Energia. Postura y movimiento.* Grupo Editorial Norma. Bogota

Russell Robert A. (1950) *You Can Too Be Prosperous Studies in Prosperity.* Devorss Publications. Camarillo CA

Ruiz Don Manuek (1997). *The Four Agreements.* Amber-Allen Publishing California

Sethi Ramit (2009) *I Will Teach You To Be Rich.* Workman Publishing New York

Seton, Julia (1972) *The Science of Success.* Health Reseach, Pomeroy WA

Silva Jose and Burt Goldman (1989) *Dinamica del Metodo Silva de Control Mental.* Vergara Diana. Buenos Aires

Skomal Lendre. (2006) *Gratitude.* Cider Mill Press Book Publishers. Kennebunkport

Smiles Samuel (1885) *Thrift, or How to Get on in the World.* Belford, Clarke and Company Chicago

Speller Jon P. (2012) *Seed Money in Action.* USA

Stanley Thomas. (2001) *The Millionaire Mind.* Andrews Mc Meel Publishing LLC Kansas

Stanley Thomas William Danko (2010) Millionaire Next Door. Taylor Trade. Publishing. UK

Stanley Thomas ( 2004) *Millionaire Women Next Door.* Mc Keel Publishing. Kansas

Stanley Thomas (2009) *Stop Acting Rich.* John Wiley and Sons. New Jersey

Stanley Thomas (2001) *The Millionaire Mind.* Andrews McMeel Publishers. Kansas

Schwartz David J. (2007) *The Magic of Thinking Big.* Simon and Schuster. Fireside New York

Schwarz Joyce (2008) *The Vision Board. The Secret to an Extraordinary Life.* Collins Design New York

Sharamon Shalila and Bodo J. Baginski. (1999) *The Chakra Handbook. From Basic Undestanding to Practical Application.* Lotus Light Application. USA

Taylor David (2010) *The Naked Millionaire.* Capstone. United Kingdom

Taylor Sandra Anne (2009) *Quantum Success. The Astounding Science of Wealth and Happiness.* Hay House. London

Trine Ralph W. (1976) *Character Building Thought Power.* Health Research. Pomeroy WA

Tolle Eckhart. *The Power of Now.* (2005) *A guide to Spiritual Enlightenment.* Hodder and Stoughton Ltd. London

Tolle Eckhart (2001) *Practising the Power of Now.* Hodder Mobius. USA

Trump Donald J., Robert T Kiyosaki and others. (2006) *Why We Want You to Be Rich. Two Men One Message.* Rich Press. USA

Twist Lynne (2003) *The Soul of Money. Reclaiming the Wealth of our Inner Resources.* W.W. Norton £ Company. New York

Vitale Joe O Fator atraccao. (2006) *Lua de papel.* Portugal

Vitale Joe (2002) *Spiritual Marketing.* Author House. USA

Vitale Joe (2003) *The Greatest Money Making in History.* Author House USA

Walmstey Bernice (2006) *Decluttering.* Hodder Education. London

Wattles Wallace (1910) *The Science of Getting Rich.* Elizabeth Towne Publishing NewYork

Webster Richard (1998) *Feng Shui for Apartment Living.* Llewellyn Publications. U.S.A

Williams Nick (2010) *The Business You Were Born to Create.* Ballonview Ltd. Kent

Wolborn Herman (1977) *Emmet Fox's Golden Keys to Successful Living and Reminiscences.* Harper and Row Publishers. New York

Yin Amora 'Quan (1996) *The Pleadian Workbook. Awakening your Divine Ka.* Bear and Company. Vermont

BOOKS

O is a symbol of the world, of oneness and unity. In different cultures it also means the "eye," symbolizing knowledge and insight. We aim to publish books that are accessible, constructive and that challenge accepted opinion, both that of academia and the "moral majority."

Our books are available in all good English language bookstores worldwide. If you don't see the book on the shelves ask the bookstore to order it for you, quoting the ISBN number and title. Alternatively you can order online (all major online retail sites carry our titles) or contact the distributor in the relevant country, listed on the copyright page.

See our website **www.o-books.net** for a full list of over 500 titles, growing by 100 a year.

And tune in to myspiritradio.com for our book review radio show, hosted by June-Elleni Laine, where you can listen to the authors discussing their books.

MySpiritRadio